Transactions
of the
American Philosophical Society
Held at Philadelphia
For Promoting Useful Knowledge
Vol. 87, Pt. 2

The Later Roman Colonate
and Freedom

Miroslava Mirković

——— •••◦●◦••• ———

AMERICAN PHILOSOPHICAL SOCIETY
INDEPENDENCE SQUARE ■ PHILADELPHIA
1997

Mirković, Miroslava, 1933-
  The later Roman Colonate and Freedom/Miroslava Mirković
  P.   Cm.--Transactions of the American Philosophical Society
ISBN: 0-87169-872-2 ; v. 87, pt. 2
  Includes bibliographical references and index.
  ISBN 0-87169-872-2 (pbk)
  1. Colonatus (Roman law)   I. Title.   II. Series
  KJA2202.m57   1997   97-907
   340.5'4-DC21   CIP

US ISSN: 0065-9746

In Memory of my Brother
Jovan
(1932-1980)

Contents

PREFACE

My research into the *coloni* of the Later Roman Empire began in 1982-1983 when I had the privilege of spending the academic year at the Institute for Advanced Study in Princeton. I continued it at intervals in the succeeding years, whenever I had the opportunity of spending some time at libraries in Rome (Das Deutsche Archaeologische Institut) Munich (Kommission für Alte Geschichte) and Bonn (Seminar für Alte Geschichte).

I started to study the question of freedom of the *coloni* — a social category struggling to survive, not to be free—in Constantine's law dating from 332, C.Th. V 17,1, which drastically restricted the freedom of this freeborn people, threatening them as slaves: the *coloni* could be placed in irons in order to oblige them to work. How this came about is certainly a complex question, especially in two aspects. The most important seemed to me to consider how much the loss of the *colonus'* liberty was the effect of state pressure and second, how much was it a result of personal culpability on the part of the *colonus*. To answer the latter it was important to discover, as far as documentary material allows, the *colonus'* own attitude toward his personal freedom, in those instances where he had to ensure not only a meager existence but survival.

I sought the answer to the question posed by Constantine's law, how the free tenant became a *servus terrae*, in various legal, papyrological, and literary texts. In the following study, I have quoted the sources in full and in the original for two reasons: first, it seemed that this is the only possible means of justifying the interpretation and second, because some sources frequently referred to, but which do not quote the original text, have gradually became points of reference within certain fields of investigation, while their actual content has been gradually lost. These texts are rarely literally translated into English in the following pages; some have been analysed and interpreted, so that literal translation seems superfluous; good English translations already exist of laws contained in the Codex Theodosianus. The same applies to editions of papyrological texts and ancient authors quoted in this book.

I must acknowledge my debt to the Institute for Advanced Study in Princeton where I finished the essential part of this study. I wish to thank to the colleages in Princeton, in Munich and Bonn, and in the Deutchen Archaeologischen Institute in Rome for their cordiality and courtesy. My greatest obligation, however, is to Professor Glen Bowersock and Professor Christian Habicht, both of whom read the manuscript. I am thankful to Professor Dennis Kehoe for many helpful suggestions. I must express my gratitude to the American Philosophical Society and the Associate Editor, Carole LeFaivre-Rochester, for printing this difficult text.

Beograd, 1997   M. Mirković

FOREWORD

The issue of freedom is fundamental to any study of the Roman colonate. The *problem* of freedom arises primarily when, in contradiction to the prevailing rules and norms of a society, it has been reduced or threatened. For slaves at the time of the Roman Empire, freedom cannot be represented as a problem since slavery in Rome, and also in Greece, was considered not only legal but natural.[1]

The liberty enjoyed by freemen found legal expression in the Roman state. Only Roman citizens could act of their own free will, the limitation to this being set by *ius* and *vis*.[2] Judging by legal texts dating from the fourth to the sixth century, the freedom of the *coloni*, as a category of the free agricultural workers, was threatened. Allusion was made to this earlier in the *Digesta* and also occurs in literary and papyrological evidence. According to some fifth-century authors, the *coloni* had lost the dignity (*dignitas*) of freemen.[3] This was not a question of political freedom—the Roman *libertas* had lost this concept with the coming of the Principat[4]—but the basic, individual liberties that separated free citizens from slaves.

The laws of the later Roman Empire point to the *colonus* as *ingenuus* and *homo liber*, doubtless because in practice there were many circumstances that contradicted this concept. In legal regulations, they were always separated from those who were *servi* or *mancipia*. In reality, however, there was a range of restrictions concerning the individual rights that separated the *coloni* from free peasants, thus relegating them to a position between free and slaves.[5]

From the sixteenth to the seventeenth century and in earlier commentaries on the Theodosian Code there is discussion as to how

---

1. Arist., Pol. I 7

2. *Dig.*I 5,4

3. Salvian, *De gub. Dei* V 43

4. Numerous contemporary studies on Roman liberty deal with its political aspect, among them Ch. Wirszubski, *Libertas as a Political Idea at Rome during the Later Republic and Early Principate* (Cambridge, 1968); J. Bleicken, *Staatliche Ordnung und Freiheit in der römischen Republik* (Frankfurt, 1972) (FAS 6) 52 ff.; O. Gigon, *Die antike Philosophie als Maasstab und Realität* (Zürich-München, 1977), 96 ff.; G.Grifò, "Remarques sur les problèmes de l'égalité et de la liberté à Rome," *Ktema* 6 (1981): 193 ff. and others. The problem of individual, personal freedom is discussed by Mommsen, *Bürgerlicher und peregrinischer Freiheitsschutz im römischen Staat, Juristische Abhandlungen*, Festgabe für Georg Beseler zum 6. Januar 1885, 253 ff. (Ges. Schr. III 1, ff.).

5. For social and juristic status of individuals, see E. Levy, ZSS 78 (1961): 169 ff.; D. Nörr, ZSS 82 (1965): 87ff.

the *coloni*, a priori free, came to a position close to that of slaves.[6] Explanations are various and theories numerous. Some of the more important among them are:

  • the colonate supposedly emerged in a natural fashion due to the gradual deterioration of the position of those who were originally tenants on others' land; debt and rent arrears made them dependent on the landowner;

  • the *colonus*'s origin in serfdom may have lain at the root of the dependence; the *coloni* were initially slaves who received part of the property of their master in order to work on it as *coloni* yielding up part of the produce and keeping part of it as *peculium* (*servi quasi coloni*).

  • the colonate may have been a phenomenon of non-Roman origin, formed of debtors in Gaul and Germaia, in Asia Minor and Illyricum (*obaerati*).

  • the colonate was imported to Roman soil; this was the position in which prisoners of war and barbarians found themselves, after migrating into Roman territory;

  • the ties binding the *coloni* to the land they tilled and the loss of the right to leave could have been the results of fiscal reform under Diocletian and other fourth-century emperors.[7]

---

6. Cujacius, as early as 1566, in his edition *of Codex Theodosianus*, endeavored to explain the origin of the Roman colonate. In his opinion, dependent *coloni* were not unknown even before Diocletian: *operarii* and *coloni*, documented in the *Digesta*, were to be recognized later in the *Codes* as *inquilini* and *coloni*. The explanation given by Gothofredus, in his edition of the Code, in 1665, was different: he was inclined to see the Roman colonate as a social phenomenon transferred to the Roman state by the barbarian *dediticii* who were settled there by the Emperor's order.

7. All theories on the Roman colonate up to the 1920s are reviewed by R.Clausing, in his book *The Roman Colonate, the theories of its origin* (New York, 1925 [1965]). For further bibliography, see M. Kaser, *Das römische Privatrecht, II Abschnitt (*1975): 141-143. Among the studies published after Clausing's book, important for studying the freedom of the *coloni* are: Ch. Saumagne, "Du role de l' 'origo' et du 'census' dans la formation du colonat romain," *Byzantion* 12 (1937): 486ff.; P. Collinet, *Le colonat dans l'Empire Romain*, Recueil de la Soc. Jean Bodin *II, Le servage,*1937, 195ff. F.Ganshof, "Le statut personnel du colon au Bas-Empire," *Ant.Class.* 14 (1945): 261ff.; A. Segrè, "The Byzantine Colonate," *Traditio* 5 (1947):103ff.; M.Palasse, *Orient et Occident à propos du colonat Romain au Bas-Empire*, 1950; A.H.M. Jones, *The Roman Colonate, Past and Present* 13 (1958): 1ff. (reprint in P.A. Brunt, *The Roman Economy*, 1974, ch.XIV, 293ff.); W. Held,"Das Ende der progressiven Entwicklung des Kolonates am Ende des 2. und in der ersten Hälfte des 3. Jhds. im römischen Imperium," *Klio* 52 (1970): 239ff.; W. Goffart, *Caput* and *Colonate, Towards a History of Later Roman Taxation* (Toronto, 1974); D. Eibach, "Untersuchungen zum spätantiken Kolonats in der kaiserlichen Gesetzgebung," Diss. (Köln, 1980); J.-M. Carrié, *Le colonat du Bas-Empire: un mythe historiographique*, Opus 1, 1982, 351ff.; idem, *Un roman des origines: les généalogies du colonat du Bas-*

Some of these theories were quite rightly abandoned early on, among them those on slave origins of the colonate, on its transfer from the Gallic and Germanic countries to the Roman state and on the dependent colonate as a status created for barbarians living on Roman territory. Others, such as the theory of indebtedness and arrears of rent as reason for the loss of independence, despite convincing arguments, have nowadays been abandoned.[8] The theory of administrative pressure and primarily fiscal reasons for binding the *colonus* to the land, although it scrutinizes only one aspect of the question, today leads the field.[9]

As far as we now know, the position of *colonus*, tied both to the landowner and the land, was occupied by freeborn tenants, slaves as tenants *(servi quasi coloni)* and finally barbarians who had either moved voluntarily into Roman territory or had been settled there as prisoners of war.

The present study concentrates on the problem of loss of freedom by those who were born free Roman citizens but who later, as *coloni*, sank to a position between freedom and slavery. The

Empire, Opus 2, 1983, 205ff.; idem, *Figures du* "colonat" *dans les papyrus d'Egypte, lexique, contextes, Atti XVII Pap. Congr.* vol. 3, 1984, 939ff.; А В Коптев, "Изменение статуса римских колонов в IV-V вв," (The change of status of Roman *coloni* in the fourth and fifth centuries A.D.), ВДИ 1989/4:33ff.; idem, " Свобода" и "рабство" колонов в Позднеи римскои империи (The "freedom" and "slavery" of the *coloni* in the Later Roman Empire), ВДИ 1990/2: 24f.; a useful collection of the literary, legal and epigraphical texts with introduction and translation in German has been published by K.P.Johne, J.Kohn and V.Weber, *Die Kolonen in Italien und in den westlichen Provinzen des römischen Reiches, eine Untersuchung der literarischen, juristischen und epigraphischen Quellen vom 2. Jahhundert v.u.Z. bis zu den Severern* (Berlin, 1983). Johne's paper entitled "Colonus, colonia, colonatus," *Philologus* 132, (1988/2): 308ff., deals with the term itself. On the following pages only theories that influenced subsequent researches will be taken into consideration. Slaves in the position of *coloni (servi quasi coloni)* are not included in the present study, their unfree status being due not to their position as *coloni* but to their slave origin (cf. P.Veyne,"Le dossier des esclaves colons remains," *Revue hist.* 315 [1981]: 3ff.).

8. As was the case with the study of Fustel de Coulanges, *Le colonat romain, Recherches sur quelques problemes d'histoire*, 1885.

9. This theory is accepted in general histories of the period, such as E. Stein's *Histoire du Bas-Empire* I, 193, or A.H.M. Jones's *The Later Roman Empire, passim*, especially p. 785f. and in recent studies of the later Roman colonate, such as W. Goffart's *Caput and Colonate, Towards a History of Late Roman Taxation* (Toronto, 1974) or D. Eibach's *Untersuchungen zum spätantiken Kolonat in der kaiserlichen Gesetzgebung* (Köln, 1976). See also recently B. Sirks, "Reconsidering the Roman Colonate," ZSS Rom. Abt. 110 (1993): 320ff. and P. Panischek, "Der spätantiken Kolonat: Eing Substitut für die 'Halbfreiheit' peregriner Rechtsetzungen?" ZSS Rom. Abt. 111 (1994), 37ff. Accepting the idea of the formal creation of the colonate by law, Panischek suggests that the colonate was created in order to define the juristic status of the semidependent people.

question of barbarians who became *coloni* on the Roman territory also merits attention. Data on barbarians as *coloni* are useful for study of the existing relationships but not of their origin, as they were absorbed into a status which already existed in the Roman state. Slaves as *coloni* are not included in this research as these were unfree by birth and this aspect therefore should be studied under the heading of slavery.[10]

The status of the *colonus* including the question of his freedom, represents as much a legal as a sociological problem. K.F. von Savigny devoted studies to the question of his legal position, particularly a work dating from 1850.[11]

According to Savigny, the colonate had three origins: a man could become a *colonus* by birth, by contract or by spending a long number of years as a tenant on the same land. He also adds punishment as another possibility. One could become a *colonus* by birth in four cases: 1) by being born of a father *colonus*— 2) mother slave, of a father freeman— 3) mother *colona*, of a father *colonus*— 4) mother free woman, or in the case of both parents being *coloni* (frequently on different properties). A long number of years *(Verjährung)* of work on the same land (thirty or more) could bring the tenant into the position of a dependent *colonus* who had lost the right to leave the land. By contract—the third method—Savigny assumes a marriage contract to which either a *colonus* or *colona* is party, or a written declaration in which the *colonus* recognizes his own status. Savigny reverts to the query as to how the parents of a *colonus* became *coloni* at the end of his article, but without insisting on an answer. Underlining the frequent mention of *coloni* in the legislation of the Constantine's time, he rejects the idea of a link with the *coloni* found in the *Digesta*. He illustrates this difference by examples taken from the tax-rolls. According to a famous passage in the *Digesta* on *professio*, L 15,4, the *colonus* at the time of the Principate was registered for taxes by the *dominus fundi* who bore the responsibility of the *coloni* on his estates. *Coloni* of the Later Empire however appear on the tax-rolls as personally registered, under their own names. *Adscripticii* in these cases would therefore be *coloni* who paid their own taxes independently. The terms *colonus* and *inquilinus* which appear in legislation after Constantine, existed before, but in quite a different form—as designating free tenants.[12]

---

10. P. Veyne, op. cit., in n.7.

11. F.C. Savigny, *Über den römischen Kolonat*, Vermischte Schriften II, Berlin 1850, 1ff. His first report on the Roman colonate in the German Akademie dates from 1822.

12. Savigny, op. cit., 45.

Savigny discusses three aspects of the colonate: 1) personal position (*persönliche Zustand*), 2) relationship to the land *(Verhältnisse des Kolonen zum Boden)* and 3) relationship to property and taxation (*Recht am Boden und Steuer).*

The *colonus* in his personal life was *ingenuus*. Among other rights was that of entering into a legal marriage. His freedom, however, was limited in that he was considered a *servus terrae*. Not even the proprietor could set a *colonus* free of his bonds to the land to which he had no rights of his own as it did not belong to him. His prevailing duty was to till the soil and give up part of the produce to the *possessor*. He had the right to property, but not to transfer it without the permission of the landowner for whom he worked. He was protected by the law because the *canon* could not be increased arbitrarily. He himself could not sue the landowner, or could only in exceptional cases. All *coloni* were obliged to pay poll tax—an obligation they carried out independently, as they were *persönlich steuerpflichtig.*

By accident of birth an individual could wind up in the position of *colonus*. Concerning the origin of the entire group (*Stamm*), Savigny is noncommittal in his conclusion and confines himself to the assumption that there must at one time have been a great number of such *coloni* whose number were therefore reduced and obstacles placed in the way of any increase. The argument that these were slaves who were given their liberty with the proviso that they must remain on the land seems a natural one to him. Simplest of all would be explanation—if it could be proved — that personal dependence (*Leibeigenschaft*) existed in the provinces even before Roman times. It might be expected that possibilities for the emancipation of the *coloni* (*Freilassung*) existed, but sources contain no mention of this.[13] The *colonus* could be free if he remained for less than thirty years (twenty for *colona*) on the same estate.

Fustel de Coulanges refers to some of these questions in a more comprehensive way.[14] He is clearly anxious to explain the origin of the colonate and his approach is as much legal as it is historical. He treats the relationship as a private and legal one, observing its development and establishing a continuity between the colonate of the later Roman Empire and *coloni* of earlier times. Fustel de Coulanges begins with the following premises: there was no law which introduced the colonate; of the forty-three laws in the *Codes* related

---

13. Idem, 4 and 37. For the possibility of manumission of dependent *coloni*, see also Fustel de Coulanges, op. cit., 35.

14. See note 8.

to the colonate, not one defines the position of the *colonus* in general; all these laws arose out of specific circumstances and in relation to other subjects and are therefore scattered throughout the *Codex Theodosianus* under various headings[15]; there is no mention of the colonatus in the legislation of the first three centuries of the Empire because at that time it did not come in contact with either the judiciary or the tax authorities. As soon as the *colonus* was allotted a place on the tax-rolls, the law began to take an interest in him. The roots of the colonate are to be found in an earlier age and Fustel de Coulanges sees three sources of its appearance: 1. free *coloni* who contracted to work for five years were reduced by debt and overdue rent to serfs bound to the land and its owner; 2. *coloni* who worked without a contract, such as those on the *saltus Burunitanus* in North Africa, remained on the land, tied by their own interests or out of habit, with no intention of leaving nor any of the part of the owner of driving them away; 3. finally, *coloni* who were either forced by their Roman masters or at their own request, were settled as *cultivateurs perpetuels*. These diverse circumstances were repeated from generation to generation until eventually in the Later Empire the *colonus* found himself inscribed on the tax-rolls. Finally, the *colonus* appears as a freeman and there is no law that confuses him with either *servi* or *mancipia*.[16]

Fustel de Coulanges categorically opposes an already existing opinion that imperial fiscal policy in the Later Roman Empire was the only reason for the emergence of the colonate.[17] His conclusion, briefly formulated and nowdays forgotten, is difficult to dispute: "*L'inscription au cens n'a pas fait les colons; mais elle a été le premier titre certain qui ait marqué officiellement leur condition; et elle a été aussi le premier point de contact que les colons aient eu avec le gouvernement imperial.*"[18] Underlying the discussion, however, is the argument that this was the first contact with the imperial administration. This might be true of Italy, but not of the provinces. The opinion of Fustel de Coulanges on the difference related to tax-paying between *coloni* of the Principate and those of the later Empire may be also discussed or even disputed. He discovers this difference in the method of inscription in the tax-rolls, a point on which Savigny backs him. According to the *Digesta*, it was the *dominus fundi* who enrolled both the *colonus* and *inquilinus* on his estate for taxation. From Diocletian onwards,

---

15. Fustel de Coulanges op. cit., 88.

16. Ibid., 87, 98-117.

17. Fustel de Coulanges has in mind the B. Heisterberkg's study, *Die Enstehung des Colonatus*, 1876.

18. Fustel de Coulanges, op. cit., 75; see also Savigny, op. cit., 98.

however, it is no longer the *dominus fundi* who gives the names of the *coloni* and slaves, but the *coloni* themselves who are personally taxed and pay the *capitatio*.[19] This statement is somewhat mitigated by Fustel de Coulanges who claims that though this was the theory, in practice landlords paid what was owed to the state by those living on their land. Lastly, in his opinion, not all *coloni* were *censiti*. There were, he thinks, several types of *coloni*, as may be seen from earlier terms such as *originarii* or *originales*— those whose families had been *coloni* for more than one generation; *censiti, adscripticii* or *tributarii* who paid poll tax, *inquilini* who were originally house tenants but later become the same as *coloni*, and finally the *coloni* who were neither *originarii* nor *adscripticii*. These terms were not synonymous nor did they mean the same person.

Although arising in various ways and therefore different, they share some characteristics: the *colonus* was a free person, in contrast to the *mancipia* and *servi*; the *nexus colonarius* was one thing, the *condicio servitutis* quite another. The *colonus* had the right to marriage and inheritance; the landowner could not sell him; he could appear in court as a witness and take holy orders. There are, however, circumstances that narrow the gap between *colonus* and *servus*. Just as the slave could not leave his master, the *colonus* could not leave the land he tilled and the landowner gradually become his master. The services were no longer open to him, not even military service. His position became hereditary. In the case of his taking holy orders or entering the army, the landowner's rights over him were first taken into account.[20]

Thus the *colonus*, although not a slave, was not free and this position was legally formulated, as for example *paene est ut quadam servitute dediti videantur* in C.J.XI 50. He could, accordingly to Fustel, remain free, if he remained on the same estate for less than 30 years.[21]

When considering colonate relationship from the later Republic to the Later Empire in Rome, Fustel de Coulanges established a continuity in development throughout several centuries. He rules out state intervention as a central factor in the creation of the colonate. The *coloni* in his opinion, really became unfree because they had lost their economic independence. At one time free, they found themselves in a situation where they could no longer leave the estate on which they lived: "Their original contract allowed this, but the rent they owed forbade it; they were not tied to the land by the law, but

---

19. Op. cit., 75-77.

20. Op. cit., 98-117.

21. Op. cit., 116.

by debt. The land held them back not because they were *coloni* but
because they were debtors."[22]

This point of view was disputed by J.-M.Carrié almost a century
later. Carrié considered that it had been inspired by a bourgeois
rationalism which regarded the colonate from a liberal ideology
perspective and that Fustel de Coulanges had contributed most to the
modern myth of the colonate. Carrié does not enter into the argu-
mentation of Fustel de Coulanges; he criticizes him for strictly ad-
hering only to the sources and he himself is prepared to defend the
generally held point of view—it appeared in the nineteenth-century
German thought—that the colonate was a product of the state
administrative pressure and that the dependence of the *colonus*, came
about due to Diocletian's fiscal reform.[23]

When he established a continuity between the earlier *coloni* and
the colonate in *Codes*, Fustel de Coulanges had in mind above all its
Italic roots. M. Rostowzew in his study about Kolonatus dated 1910[24]

---

22. Op. cit., 18.

23. J.-M. Carrié, "Le colonat du Bas-Empire: un mythe historiographique?" *Opus* 1,
(1982): 352ff. disputes the following assumptions of Fustel de Coulanges: the
establishment of any continuity in the development of social and economic
formation from the Roman Empire to the ninth century; the consideration of the
conditions of the colonate from the perspective of a liberal ideology, *a)* that the
colonate was already in existence when the state took an interest in it for fiscal
reasons and *b)* that the binding of the *colonus* to the soil he cultivated was a product
of the *"rapport contractuel."* By defending the spontaneous nature of the appearance
of the colonate, Fustel de Coulanges, as Carrié thinks, was in fact recognizing a
custom as a source of authority and a factor of historic evolution: as a freeman, the
colonus was not subjugated to the state but to another man; Fustel was confusing
public and private law, here between the ideas of "fixation fiscale and the contractual
régime of land exploitation;" he did not recognize the right of the state to regulate
the economic relations of the group to which he opposed self-regulation instead.
Although the colonate, in Fustel's opinion, was not a reality introduced by law, it
was recognized in order to prevent abuse or attacks on the principles of personal
rights.
    Carrié was to return to some of these questions in his paper "Un roman des
origines: les généalogies du colonat du Bas-Empire," *Opus* 2 (1983): 205ff. This in turn
was to be disputed by A.Marcone, "Il colonato del tardo impero: un mito
storiografico?" *Athenaeum* (1985): 513ff., who focused his criticism mainly on the
question of continuity, the chronological and geographical universality of the
colonate and the issue of the position of the *colonus* as a category between freeman
and slave. In any case, it is essential to return to the sources, which in many cases
confirm the general point of view of Fustel de Coulanges. On his value, see also M.
Finley, "Masters and Slaves," in *The Ancient Economy*, (1973), 70: "Fustel's argument
has attached little attention because historians have been too obsessed with the evils
of slavery to appreciate the evils of short-term tenancy under the harsh Roman law
of debt. The argument is no less valid for this neglect."

24. M. Rostowzew, "Studien zur Geschichte des römischen Kolonates," *Archiv für*

also insists on the general in the development of this institution, but sets out from the aspect of Hellenistic administration in Egypt and other eastern countries. The Romans only continued the policy of the Ptolemies and Seleucids. He thus shifted the question of continuity into the sphere of influence of the Hellenistic countries on Rome. In his research he does not go further than the third century A.D.

Later studies of the colonate tend to be dominated by the point of view that it was created by administrative pressure, particularly the fiscal policy of Diocletian and fourth-century emperors. This theory arose in the 1850s and frequently appears in works of the time. Most modern works also incline in this direction. C. Saumagne,[25] in his study dated 1937, considers that two types of *coloni* existed at the time of the Principate; *coloni* and *inquilini*. This idea is primarily based on the inscription from Henchir Metich in North Africa, that shows that both, a) *coloni* who had *villae dominicae* and who were *in fundo* and b) those who were *ultra fundo, inquilini* in his opinion, worked on lands belonging to the emperor.[26] Both terms were retained in the Later Roman Empire: the *colonus* of the earlier period became the *adscripticius* or *tributarius* after Diocletian. Saumagne designates the first as *colonus₁* while the former *inquilinus* took on the meaning originally held by the *colonus* and is also given the designation *colonus₂*. From the end of the fourth century they exist as two classes: one subjected to the *conditio tributaria* and entering into the *capitatio humana* taxation system, while the other is in a more favorable position and free of the *capitatio*. Both, however, were obliged to remain on the land they tilled and were subject to the *ius originarium*. The freedom of the *tributarius* was restricted, in his opinion, by the *capitatio;* those who were not *tributarii* had *ingenuitas* and although obliged to remain on the land, merited the title of free men, in relation to the others. From the late fourth century, both classes were in the same position as far as inheritance of this status was concerned.[27]

The study of Saumagne, abstract for the most part and inclined to generalized conclusions, has attracted less attention than it deserves. His pivotal point of departure and indisputable conclusion is:

Papyrusforschung, (Beiheft 1.1910).

25. Ch. Saumagne, "Du role de l' 'origo' et du 'census' dans la formation du colonat romain," *Byzantion* 12 (1937): 487ff.

26. CIL VIII 25902, line I 6. For this and other North African inscriptions, see J. Kolendo, "Le colonat en Afrique sous le Haut-Empire," *Centre de recherches d' histoire ancienne 17, Annales litteraires de l' Université de Besançon,* (1977); D. Flach, *Chiron* 8 (1978,) 441ff.

27. Saumagne, op. cit., 493ff.; 508f.

tributarii or *adscripticii* were enrolled in the *census* of a given estate and paid their *capitatio* through the *dominus fundi*.[28] Here Saumagne differs fundamentally from Fustel de Coulanges who considered that it was in fact the *adscripticii* who enrolled under their own names in the *libri censuales* at the time of the Later Roman Empire and paid their own *capitatio*. This conclusion, however, was lost in a welter of other, less appropriate ones, among which were those that tried to attribute the emergence of the *colonus'* dependence to administrative pressure. By giving the *dominus fundi* the right to collect tax, the state then transferred to him the right to the property of the tax debtor, which was forfeit in the case of tax debts according to an ancient regulation in the Roman state. This right of the landowner would then become the instrument by which he would acquire personal power over the *colonus*.[29]

Ganshof belatedly pointed out the credit due to Saumagne in a short work dated 1945, but disputed his identification of the *inquilinus* with the *colonus* in the later Roman legislation and the conclusion that only the *adscripticius* was subject to the *dominus fundi* while the *inquilinus* was not. He himself concludes that from the middle of the fourth century all *coloni*, because of the *ius census* were in a position close to that of slavery. He nonetheless admits that the *ius census* was felt more strongly by the *adscripticius* in subjugating him to the landowner than it was by the other *coloni*.[30]

A.H.M. Jones also supports the idea that Diocletian's fiscal reforms brought in the tying of the *colonus* to the land. This is explained in detail in his study of 1957.[31] While admitting that there were earlier allusions to *coloni* being tied to the land in some cases (North African inscriptions, inscription from Lydia), he considers the first clear and unambiguous evidence that the *coloni* (or some *coloni*) were dependent on the landowner to be Constantine's law dated 332, C.Th.V 17,1 and the first evidence of the hereditary character of the bond to be the law of 364, C.J.XI 68,3. There were *coloni* who lived on estates as land tenants and *inquilini* who were house tenants, but who worked on the estate as craftsmen or farm laborers to earn their living. There are two laws on which Jones bases his view of the dependence of the *colonus* that on the Thracian coloni,

28. Op. cit., 496ff.; 571f.

29. Ibid., 571f.; 573.

30. L. Ganshof, "Le statut personnel du colon au Bas-Empire, observations en marge d'une théorie *nouvelle*," *Ant. Class* 14 (1945): 261ff.

31. A.H.M. Jones, "The Roman Colonate," *Past and Present* 13 (1957): 1ff. (reprinted in P.A. Brunt, *The Roman Economy*, (1974,) ch.XV p.293ff.) and *LRE* II 799f.

C.J.XI 52 and that on the Illyrian *coloni*, C.J.XI 53. In the former, even after the abolition of the *capitatio*, the *coloni* did not have the right to leave the land; in the latter, they were bound to the land *nomine et titulo colonorum*. The measures binding the *coloni* to the land did not, in his opinion, precede Diocletian's time and were linked to the reorganization of the poll tax. This was primarily a fiscal measure; the binding of the *colonus* to the land would then be a by-product of more wide-ranging fiscal and administrative measures. Not only the *coloni* but peasant proprietors, too, were tied to the place of their tax registration. These measures, however, did not have the same effect everywhere. The Palaestinian *coloni* were bound to the land only in the time of Theodosius, while those in Egypt were free up to the fifth century. Finally, Jones concludes that not all *coloni* were tied to the land but only the descendants of those who had been enrolled in Diocletian's *census*. In time their numbers were reduced and their places taken by free *coloni*.[32]

Interpreting the emergence to the later Roman colonate, with *coloni* bound or tied to the soil as a consequence of Diocletian's fiscal policy, A.H.M. Jones completely ignores the relationship of the *colonus* to the *dominus fundi*. This is also characteristic of more recent works on the colonate by W. Goffart and D. Eibach. Goffart treats this aspect as so unimportant that he even considers the *coloni iuris alieni*, referred to in Constantine law of 332, to be free tenants who paid their own taxes independently and entered into contract leases of their own free will. The *dominus fundi* is lost sight of in this research and becomes a minor factor. The binding of the colonus to the land came about, in Goffart's opinion, in the late fourth century. He views the problem rather simplistically, solving it by the assumption that there was a change in the taxation pattern. In the early fourth century, individuals would have their tax assessed on the basis of their property; at the end of the century, this was done on the basis of property declared. The *colonus* was then erased from the *capita* list and registered in the tax-rolls together with the land he tilled.[33]

If A.H.M. Jones avoids giving a clear definition of the tied *colonus*, it is because it can be hardly conform to the given or inferred meaning of earlier terms used in the legislation of the fourth to sixth centuries as are: *adscripticius, originarius* and *originalis, inquilinus* and *tributarius*. In his voluminous work, *The Later Roman Empire*, Jones is inclined to interpret some of these as titles for various aspects of the

---

32. "The Roman Colonate," 297 and 301.

33. W. Goffart, *Caput and Colonate, Towards a History of Later Roman Taxation*, 1974, especially ch. V, p. 71ff.

same phenomenon.[34]

D. Eibach in his dissertation "*Untersuchungen zum spätantiken Kolonat in der kaiserlichen Gesetzgebung*," of 1976, was the first to give a systematic review of the terms in later Roman legislation related to the *coloni*: *censibus adscripti* and *adscripticii*, *originales* and *originarii*, *tributarii* and *inquilini*. His research is confined to the period from Diocletian to Justinian, ca. from 300 to 565 A.D. Two negative conclusions emerge from this study: 1. the terms quoted above are not synonymous; with the exception of *colonus* and *adscripticius*, they appear only in laws of the fourth and fifth century. Before the sixth century, terminology is reduced to two names: *colonus* μισθότός and *adscripticius* (ἐναπόγραφος). *Colonus* in the sixth century has a much wider meaning than in the preceding ones. 2. The legislature uses these terms less frequently to designate special classes of the farm-laborer population. Eibach sees more of a difference in the chronological interchange of terms used by the imperial administration.

If the formation of a dependent colonate and the binding of the *colonus* to the land are interpreted as being solely a consequence of fiscal policy on the part of the later emperors, the *dominus fundi* becomes an unimportant factor. He cannot, however, be eliminated or ignored in research for the simple reason that the laws referring to the *coloni* do not ignore him. In regulating questions of tax payment and preventing *coloni* from running away, the landowner was frequently a key factor. For this very reason, that *coloni* worked not on their own land but on that of others, special regulations were devoted to them in the laws governing the fiscal obligations of the rural population. Any attempt to study the peculiarities of the *coloni* who were more tied to their farms than peasant freeholders, leads inevitably to the relationship between the *colonus* and the landowner.

When the emergence of a dependent colonate is interpreted as a by-product of Diocletian's fiscal policy, the underlying belief is that the later Roman Empire was repressive and that it was therefore possible by an act of the imperial chancellory to render at one stroke an entire class immobile and tied to the land. Recent studies, however, indicate that the repressive character of the later Roman state is questionable.[35] The theory that one of Diocletian's laws bound to the

---

34. *LRE* II 799.

35. The theory of continuity in the development of the colonate, from the first century B.C. to the Later Roman Empire did not find many followers. The *coloni* of the Later Republic and the Early Empire are treated by modern scholars as a phenomenon different from the colonate after Diocletian. See for example Kolendo, op. cit. in note 26; P.W. de Neeve, *Colonus, private farm tenancy in Roman Italy during the Republic and the Early Principate* (Amsterdam, 1982).

rural population to their farms also has its weaknesses. The emperor is not cited as author of any such law in any of the later rescripts referring to the *coloni*, taxation or escape from the land. This is quite striking in the light of the fact that some emperors from the fourth to the sixth century refer to the regulation of their predecessors as Justinian does to Anastasius in his law of the application of the same rule to *liberi coloni* after 30 years period as to the dependent *coloni* or simply to the *lex a maioribus constituta* in order to lend weight to his edicts. Another difficulty is that the majority of laws restricting the freedom of the *coloni* date from the second half of the fourth century, so that some are a century younger than Diocletian. Laws of this kind, directed from the imperial administration to Thrace and Illyricum as well as the law of the Palaestinian *coloni* are not of the same date .

The freedom of the *coloni* could have been threatened by his tax obligations, but it would seem that this was not the only nor the most important feature of his position. An undoubtedly important question is the relationship between the *colonus*, as a man working on another's land toward the person who owned it.[36] In the Later Roman Empire, as before, it was primarily on the *colonus* to cultivate the land and pay to the landowner. Even in discussing the fiscal obligations of the *coloni*, the *dominus fundi*, through whose mediation many *coloni* paid their taxes, cannot be ignored.

It is difficult to foresee any reconciliation of the two theories, one of the colonate as a by-product of the fiscal policy of fourth-century emperors, the other of a previously created dependence on the landowner, but it is possible to discuss the extent to which one factor or the other diminished the freedom of the *colonus*: what the role of the central imperial administration was in bringing about the dependence of the *coloni* and what the consequence of the private and legal relationship between the tenant and landowner was. Linked to this is the question whether the *coloni* as a social category lost their freedom or whether it was individuals who, by losing the economic

---

36. Tax payment could be, as many papyrological documents reveal, the subject of a contract between tenants and proprietor. Indirect payment of taxes through the landlord is not necessarily peculiar to the Later Roman Empire. Even in the second and third centuries there were tenants who paid their taxes indirectly and who were treated as a special class in Egyptian documents. See P. Wessely Prag., published in *Eunomia, Listy filologické* 5, 80 (1957): 1, pp. 16-31 and 2, pp. 56-80; cf. L. Varcl, "Μετρηματίαοι," *JJP* 11/12 (1957/8): 97ff. For the character of the Later Roman state, see R. MacMullen, "Social mobility and the Theodosian Code," *JRS* 54 (1964): 49ff.; H.J. Horstkotte, "Die Theorie von spätantiken "Zwangstaat" und das Problem der Steuerhaftung," *Beiträge zur klassischen Philologie* 159 (1984); D.W. Rathbone, in Atti del colloquio intern. *The Ancient Economy and Greco-Roman Egypt*, (Bologna, 1987 [1989]), 161f.; idem, *Economic Rationalism and Rural Society in third-century A.D. Egypt.*

independence, were forced to give up part of their personal freedom.

The opinion that the *coloni* as a class lost their freedom to leave the land they tilled and some individual rights and found themselves in a position between free and slaves, is weakened by the circumstance that in the laws up to the time of Justinian, those who remained free, *liberi coloni*, appear beside obviously dependent *coloni*.

Laws from the fourth to the sixth century regulating the cases of escaped *coloni* and their punishment, on the transfer of tax liability to the person sheltering the fugitive, on the rights of the *dominus fundi* for whom the *colonus* worked and so on, reveal one side of the problem: the extent to which fiscal policy in the later Roman Empire contributed to the binding of the *coloni* to the land and its owner and therefore to the diminishment of their freedom. The dependence of the *colonus* has another side, related to the private and legal relationship between the person cultivating land that did not belong to him and the owner of that land. There are two points of access to the study of this relationship which certainly existed prior to Diocletian: one leads to sources of the colonate in the time preceding Diocletian, the other to papyrological sources, primarily those on ἐναπόγραφοι or *adscripticii* and legal texts. Papyrological evidence, particularly from the period between the fourth and sixth centuries, contemporaries of the legal texts contained in Codes, are not evidence of the application of these laws in Egyptian practice, but on the relationship between ἐναπόγραφος and δεσπότης. They therefore reveal a side of the problem not dealt with by the law. There is no real reason here to believe in any particularly different Egyptian development.[37] That the term ἐναπόγραφος—the same as that used for *adscripticius* in Greek version of sixth-century laws—regularly appears in the papyrological documents, shows that in this sphere the same laws were in force in Egypt as in the other provinces. There is no real reason either to single out any other region. The Latin *adscripticius* as a term corresponding to the Greek ἐναπόγραφος has been confirmed by an inscription from Asia Minor.[38]

Later Roman legislation does not go into the question of the conditions of leases or the obligations of *coloni* proceeding therefrom. Like other sources, they do not explain the emergence of the colonate. It had been in existence for a long time already and probably throughout the Roman state. Both laws and other documentary texts, particularly papyrological, as well as data from ancient authors, reveal

---

37. See N. Lewis, "The Romanity of Roman Egypt," *Atti XVI* Pap. Kongr. 3 (1984): 1077ff.; J.G. Keenan, "On Law and Society in the Later Roman Egypt," *ZPE* 17 (1975): 237ff.

38. CIL III 13640.

that there were various categories of *coloni*. Basically, some were considered to be free—*liberi coloni*—and other dependent, *coloni iuris alieni*. This difference was not brought about by Diocletian's fiscal system, but it made use of it and contributed to entrenching it. The fiscal policy of fourth-century emperors certainly deserve attention but the relationship between *colonus* and *possessor*, which is indubitably much older than the first laws on *coloni* and which is taken into account by them, cannot be ignored.

* * *

The aim of the research combined in this study under the title "The Later Roman Colonate and Freedom" is not to create a new theory of the origin of the colonate, but to show the circumstances surrounding it and to discover to what measure these contributed to reducing free tenants to a position where they did not dare to leave the land they tilled, land which did not belong to them. What is at issue here, is the freedom of common people who worked another's land in order to survive. This freedom has no political aspect. Two things emerge as significant in studying the question of freedom among *coloni* in the later Roman Empire: 1. the *colonus* and his fiscal obligation, 2. the relation of the *colonus* to the landowner, which certainly predated his relations toward taxation. As both, the fiscal system and individual indebtedness have a bearing on the origin of the *colonus'* dependence and gradual loss of freedom, both aspects have been included in the following studies. The effect of the fiscal system has been studied from example of a numerous and, it could be said, composite group of *homologi* that include both *coloni* and free, taxable peasants. The position of dependent *coloni* is best illustrated by the example of *adscripticii*. Consideration has also been given to the *inquilini* who could have become dependent and to barbarians settled on Roman territory and included in the existing category of dependent *coloni* by an imperial decision, as if they were *adscripticii*. Other terms applied to dependent *coloni* such as *censiti, tributarii, originales* and *originarii*, the Greek terms ὑπόφορος and ὑπεύθινος, as they did not designate special groups, have not been given separate chapters. They are primarily additional qualifiers or even synonyms for one of the existing groups, under the heading of tax (*censiti, tributarii,* ὑπόφοροι), or origin (*originarii, originales*) or are comprehensive terms which may be applied either to dependent people, as ὑπεύθινος, or to both, as *colonus* (γεωργός).

In fact, one can only speak either of free *coloni* with no debts to *dominus fundi*, the *liberi coloni* in the law texts, and those reduced by debt to dependence, the *coloni iuris alieni*.

Discussion of *coloni* who were *iuris alieni* seems crucial to research into the question of freedom and so it is allotted a separate chapter which to a certain extent also sums up the study of various groups.

TAX AND FREEDOM

Numerous theories on the origin of the dependent colonate in contemporary thought may actually be reduced to two theories of research: those who claim that *coloni* sank gradually into a position of quasi-slavery due to rent arrears, i.e. because of the private debt to the land proprietor, and those who explain the dependence of the *coloni* as the result of Diocletian's fiscal reform, the severity of which was rooted in the idea that those who tilled the land did not have the right to leave it.

The two theories on the origin of the dependent colonate are mutually exclusive: debts and indebtness belong to the sphere of private law— the dependence of individuals originating with the one to whom the land belonged, while on the other hand the rigidity of fiscal obligations thus conceived led to the dependence of entire groups on the state. Dependence of the *colonus* to the *dominus fundi,* however, appears in later empire laws concerning taxation and fiscal duties. Both aspects, therefore, merit attention, in general and in relation to individual groups of *coloni* mentioned in the laws or other sources, when considering the problem of diminished freedom of the *coloni.* Born free, they lost part of their freedom working on land that did not belong to them.

Since the mid-nineteenth century, the tendency has been to explain the dependence of the later Roman colonate as a consequence of administrative pressure. Revillout narrowed this down to the issue of taxation and some researchers in the latter half of this century continued this argument, emphasizing the part played by Diocletian's fiscal reform in binding the *colonus* to the land.[1] The majority of recent works, whether general histories of the later Roman state or studies devoted exclusively to this problem, treat the dependent colonate of the fourth to sixth centuries as a new phenomenon and a

---

1. Ch. Revillout, "Etude sur l'histoire du colonat chez les Romains," *Revue hist. de droit français et etrang.* 2 (1856):417ff. and the same 3 (1857):209ff. D. Serrigny in his *Droit public et administratif romain,* (1862) II, 386, was the first to discover the difference between serf *coloni* and free *coloni.* It seems important to note also Heisterbergk's opinion, *Die Enstehung des Colonatus,* (1876) that the origin of the colonate is to be sought in the provinces, not in Italy. According to him, the basic reason for the transformation of free tenants into dependent *coloni* bound to the soil, was Diocletian's fiscal reform. For other early theories on the origin of the colonate, see Clausing, *Colonate,* especially 91-137, chapter "Administrative pressure."

legal creation, a consequence of Diocletian's fiscal reform.[2]

There is no doubt that there was a striking tendency in Later
Roman Empire legislation to prevent the rural population from
leaving the land. Fiscal objectives were clearly delineated in all laws
related to the problem. The first question is: was this a new departure
of the Later Empire after Diocletian; the second and clearly more
complex question is whether the tax system could reduce the *coloni,*
more than other categories working the land, to a state of dependence while depriving them of the possibility of leaving, when they so
desired, the land they did not own. In post–Diocletian laws, they are
treated as a separate group. The reason is certainly that they worked
on land which did not belong to them, while the problem for the
Roman state was how to prevent them, without applying force, from
leaving the land, which uncultivated, would be therefore untaxable.

The answer to the first question may be sought in sources on
earlier Roman practice in the provinces. It is true that in the last
centuries of the Roman state leaving the place where one was
registered in the tax-rolls together with the land one tilled was prohibited. But it could be hardly the specific feature of the Later Roman
Empire. A system of taxation based on a census of land and people as
a work-force on it was no novelty at the time of Diocletian; earlier
information tells us of its existence in the provinces. Though not
neglected in earlier research, it is disregarded in the conclusions.

The duty to register people who worked the land *(aratores)* and
the land being cultivated (*iugera*) existed in the oldest of the Roman
provinces, in Sicily. According to Cicero, *In Verr.* II 3,120, this
practice was borrowed from Hieron's taxation system: *Lege Hieronica
numerus aratorum quotannis apud magistratus publice subscribitur.* A
professio iugerum was also carried out.[3] At the time of Verres's
governorship in Sicily, declaring an erroneous number of *iugera* was

---

2. See Jones, *Colonate,* 299: "It would seem, then, that the tying of the *colonus* to his
farm was the by-product of the fiscal and administrative measure of the wider scope,"
but he admits too, that "for such a measure there were partial and local precedents
from the principate." See also his study "Capitatio and iugatio," *JRS* 47 (1957): 88
and "Census records of the Later Roman Empire," *JRS* 43 (1983):228ff. Similar
opinion: Stein, *Bas empire, 75.* For the history of modern theories on taxation, see
A. Déléage, *La capitation du Bas-Empire,*1945, "Introduction," 5-22.

3. See Habermehl, RE VIII A-2, 1959, col. 1576; Cic. *In Verr.*II 3, 120: *Lege Hieronica numerus aratorum quotannis apud magistratus publice subscribitur.* Cf. also II
3, 21. See M. Mirković, "Zbornik Filozofskog fakulteta," *Beograd* XV-1(1975): 65ff.
(in Serbian, with an English summary, "Cicero, In Verrem III 22, 55 and the false tax
declaration").

cause for the accusation and punishment of Xenon from Maenae.

Numerous Egyptian papyrological texts testify to the effect of the taxation system on freedom of movement among the rural population. As far back as the Early Empire, restrictions were as follows: no one who worked the land and paid taxes was allowed to leave his *idia*, the place where he was registered in the tax-rolls; a tax debt could land him in prison. Leaving the land was considered illegal, as amply demonstrated by data from the first century A.D. on the *anachoresis*.[4] A frequent reason for leaving was the tax burden. According to the testimony of Philo Judaeus, tax debts deprived people of their property and frequently threatened their personal freedom.[5] Villages in the early centuries of the Roman Empire were already being abandoned for this reason. Governors of Egypt tried to return all those who had fled elsewhere.[6]

As far as responsibility for the payment of tax was concerned, the Roman state at the time of the Principate invariably held the landowner liable, regardless of whether he himself cultivated the land or this was done for him by *coloni*. This is illustrated by the example of Xenon from Maenae in Sicily, of whom Cicero, *In Verr.* III 22, 55 has the following to report: accused by Verres of having a greater number of *iugera* than he had declared, Xenon defended himself by saying that he did not cultivate the land himself, but had given it over to a *colonus*; the latter however had left the land and fled, being no longer able to endure the ill-treatment and abuse of the *decumani* who

---

4. The problem of *anachoresis* was often discussed, see for example M. Rostowzew, *Kolonatus*, 209; H. Henne, *Documents et travaux sur l'Anachoresis*, Akten VII Pap. Congr. Wien 1955; A. Boak and H. Youtie, *Flight and oppression in fourth-century Egypt*, Studi in onore di Aristide Calderini e Roberto Paribeni II, 1957, 225ff. and above all H. Braunert, *Binnenwanderung. Studien zur sozialgeschichte Ägyptens in der Ptolemaeer- and Kaiserzeit*, 1964 and his paper in *JJP* 9/10 (1955/1956): 211ff. Cf. M. Mirković, "Flucht der Bauern, Fiscal- und Privatschulden," Festgabe für Professor Johannes Straub (1989):147ff.

5. Philo Iud. *De spec. leg.* III 163: ἀλλ' οὐδὲν θαυμαστὸν οἱ φορολογίας ἕνεκα βάρβαροι τὰς φύσεις ἡμέρου παιδείας ἀγεύσται...οὐ μόνον ἐκ τῶν οὐσίων ἀλλὰ καὶ ἐκ τῶν σωμάτων ἄχρι καὶ ψυχῆς τοὺς κινδίνους ἐπιφέροντες. U. Wilcken, *Ein dunkles Blatt aus der inneren Geschichte Ägyptens*, Festschrift Hirschfeld, 1903, 123ff. explains the flight of people from the land as the result of an extraordinary situation, in this case plague, while admitting, however, that the reason might also to be burden of liturgies and taxation.

6. The follower edicts are known: W.Chr. 202 (Vibius Maximus, A.D. 104); BGU II 372 = W.Chr.19 (Sempronius Liberalis, A.D. 145); D.J.Crawford - P.E.Easterling, *JEA* 55 (1969):188 (A.D. 200/201); P. Catt. 2 = SB I 4284 (A.D.207); BGU I 159 = W.Chr. 408 (Valerius Datus, A.D. 216). See Wilcken, *Grundzüge*, p.325; Braunert, *Binnenwanderung, passim*; J.D.Thomas, *JEA* 61 (1975): 201ff.

acted as tax collectors. Cicero condemns Verres and defends Xenon. Nonetheless, the charge by itself was founded on the concept that the landlord was responsible both for making a truthful tax declaration and for paying tax. Unconvincing as Cicero's argument for the defense may sound, it reveals the following: payment of taxes could probably be transferred to the *colonus* by a lease contract; in the case of his leaving the land, however, the owner was obliged to pay off fiscal debt to the Roman state. The case of Xenon therefore is not a well-chosen illustration of an abuse of power on the part of Verres; he was simply following the usual practice.[7] If it was true that the *colonus* was cultivating undeclared *iugera*, Xenon should have said so in his *professio*. The law had envisaged this, as may be seen in a later law, *Digesta* L 15,4 (Ulpian), regulating the declaration of land and the work-force on it. First, an exact description of the estate and its boundaries had to be given, followed by what was to be sown on it for the next ten years and finally, the responsibility of the owner for the declaration of laborers was underlined: *Si quis inquilinum vel colonum non fuerit professus, vinculis censualibus tenetur*—he who does not declare an *inquilinus* or a *colonus* is himself liable for the tax.

In Egypt, too, taxation could be transferred to the tenant, to the one who did the sowing; but here too, in the case of his leaving the land, the tax debt remained with the owner. If the latter in turn were to leave the land, the burden of paying tax on it would fall to the others left in the village.[8]

Judging by written sources from Egypt—there is no real reason to believe that it was treated differently from the other provinces—the Roman state in the first three centuries endeavored to return to their *idia* all those who had fled elsewhere. The use of force was frowned on when returning a fugitive, τὰ βίαια καὶ τὰ ἄνομα, according to a text dating from 207 A.D.[9]— a recommendation also found in a fourth-century law.[10] There is no information from the Early Empire,

---

7. See Habermehl, op. cit., in n.3.

8. For Μερισμὸς ἀνακεωρεκότων, see Sh. Wallace,"Taxation in Egypt," (1938): 105ff.; Braunert, *Binnenwanderung*, passim.

9. P. Catt. 2 = SB I 4284: ἠθέλησαν καὶ τοὺς ἐν ἀλλοδαπῇ διατρίβοντας πάντας κατιέναι εἴς τὴν ἰδίαν οἰκείαν ἐκκόψαντες τὰ βίαια [καὶ ἄν]-ομα καὶ κατὰ τὰς ἱερὰς αὐτῶν ἐν[κελεύ]σεις κατεισήλθειν.- For *idia* see Braunert, *Binnenwanderung*, passim and *JJP* 11/12: 211ff. For *origo* and the link between *idia* and *origo* see D. Nörr, RE Suppl. X, 1957, 447 f.; Braunert, *Binnenwanderung*, 305 and passim.

10. C.J.XI 48,8.

however, that would prove that the Roman administration helped landowners to recover runaway *coloni*, regardless of how the question of taxation was regulated in the lease. This was obviously left up to the *possessor* and the *colonus*, as the subject of a private agreement. There were attempts to represent private debts, most likely to the landowner, as tax and state debts, in order to ensure state intervention in dunning the debtor. Ti. Iulius Alexander, the governor of Egypt at the time of Nero, expressly forbade this in his well-known edict, emphasizing that prison was penalty only for tax debts .[11]

Diocletian's fiscal system is one of the problems most frequently discussed by scholars. What is certain is that the taxation of land together with the work-force on it lay at the heart of the system. Lactantius reports the strict and detailed *census* of one and the another;[12] it is also preserved in the edict of 297 A.D. by the governor of Egypt, Aristius Optatus, ordering a *census*:

πόσα οὖν ἑκάστῃ ἀρούρᾳ πρὸς τὴν ποιότητα τῆς γῆς
ἐπεβλήθη καὶ πόσα ἑκάστῃ κεφαλῇ τῶν ἀγροικῶν
καὶ ἀπὸ ποίας ἡλικείας μεχ[ρ]ει π[ο]ίας ἀπὸ τοῦ
προτεθέντων θείου διατάγματος.[13]

Land without laborers on it could not be cultivated, neither could it be taxed; the number of *iugera* accordingly depended on the number of *capita* declared by the individual in his tax *professio.* This number included, besides the landowner and adult members of his family, those to whom the land did not belong, *coloni* and *inquilini.* The owner was, as in earlier times, in the first place liable for tax; it was he who was also, as he had been earlier, liable for the tax of all those who worked his land, as already laid down in the *Digesta,* L 15,4. Direct evidence of both is to be found in laws dating from the fourth to the fifth centuries. In a law of 366 A.D., C.Th.1,14 (C.J.XI 48,4) this long-valid principle is formulated as follows:

*Sane quibus terrarum erit quantulacumque possessio qui in suis
conscripti locis proprio nomine libris censualibus detinentur, ab
huius praecepti communione discernimus; eos enim convenit*

---

11. OGIS n.669, 2 = FIRA n.69.

12. Lact. *De mort. persec.* c. 23. On Diocletian and his fiscal reform, see T.D. Barnes, *The New Empire of Diocletian and Constantine,* (1982).

13. A.E.R. Boak and H.C. Youtie, *The Archive of Aurelius Isidorus,* (Ann Arbor 1980), 23ff. and 26f. (the Edict of Aristius Optatus).

propriae commissos mediocritati annonarias functiones sub solito exactore cognoscere.

The exclusive liability of the landowner for tax is underlined also at the time of Justinian, *Novella* 128,14: *Nullus autem penitus molestetur pro tributis terrarum quas non possidet.* The law of 366 A.D., quoted above, establishes in the same unambiguous manner the landowner's responsibility for taxation of his *colonus: Penes quos fundorum dominia sunt, pro his colonis originalibus quos in locis isdem censos esse constabit vel per se vel per actores proprios recepta compulsionis sollicitudine implenda munia functionis agnoscat.*

In the first place this type of tax system bound those to whom the land belonged to their birthplace and to *idia.* The system, however, concealed a difficulty which was to become evident in the centuries to come: how to keep the landless on the land and how to claim the *capitatio* from those who had no *iugera.*

A series of laws appeared in the seventies and nineties of the fourth century calling on all those who left the land, *liberi plebei* and *coloni* alike, to return.[14] The recovery of fugitives was the duty of the provincial governor, as seen from C.J.XI 48,8. These laws did not envisage penalties for the runaways, regardless of whether they were free *plebei* and *coloni* or dependent *coloni* and *inquilini. Plebei* and *liberi* were returned to where they came from; *coloni iuris alieni* were returned to those to whom they belonged, *cuius se esse profitetur,* as formulated in C.Th.X 12,2,2. Those who had sheltered freeborn refugees on their land were also exempt from any penalty, C.Th.cit.: *Quisquis autem plebeium se adserit esse vel liberum, fide rei ostensa ab omni molestia vindicetur et ad ea loca, ex quibus eum esse claruerit, remitatur.* If it was a freeborn farmer who had his own possession, he would be charged tax, as also would a free *colonus* who disposed of his own *peculium.*[15] If someone, however, took in another's *colonus,* one who was *alieni iuris,* he was obliged to return him and to pay tax for the time the latter had spent in his estate; in some cases, a fine would be incurred.[16] The legal reason for this penalty existed only in the case

---

14. C.Th. X 12, 2; C.J.XI 48,6; XI 53,1.

15. C.J XI 48,8, where debts are treated as a matter of private contract.

16. *Capitationem temporis agnoscant* in C.Th. V 17, 1; *indemnitatem sarciat tributorm* in C.Th. X 12, 2. The fine: C.Th. V 17, 2, A.D. 386: *Quisquis colonum iuris alieni aut sollicitatione susceperit aut occultatione celaverit, pro eo qui privatus erit, sex auri uncias, pro eo qui patrimonialis libram auri cogatur inferre;* C.J.XI 52 (Theodosius): *Si quis vero alienum colonum suscipiendum retinendumque crediderit*

of tax evasion: the *colonus* had not been working where he had been registered in the tax-rolls, together with the land and under the name of the landowner, but on the estate of the person to whom he had fled. There he appeared as an undeclared *caput*.[17]

The legislator who provides for the return of a *colonus* to the person to whom he belongs, takes fiscal interests into account, but does not base the law on his tax liability, emphasizing instead his obligation toward the landowner. This was definitely the subject of a private contract. When the two components of the Later Roman fiscal system, *capitatio* and *iugatio*, were separated and the former was abolished, as in Thace in the time of Theodosius,[18] the legal connection between the landless and taxation disappeared also. They should have been able to leave the land and go wherever they pleased, but this in turn would raise the question of taxation based on the *iugatio terrena*. The Roman state then had recourse to an indirect method of retaining the *coloni*—authorizing the landowner to prevent them from leaving, in his capacity of *dominus* and *patronus, et patroni sollicitudine et domini potestate,* so that, freed of the burden of taxes, they would not wander about unemployed, settling wherever they wished.

Granting the landowner the legal right to retain *coloni*, whatever their fiscal liability, represents a major change in later Roman legislation. This practice was unknown in previous centuries. Neither Cicero's data on Sicily nor Egyptian papyri yield a trace on any such authority granted to landowners, although it was they who were ultimately liable for tax. If a *colonus* in the time of Principate left an estate, it was easy for the landowner to find another. In the Later Roman Empire the shortage of labor became a serious problem. The fiscal system could continue to function as it had hitherto only if all who had been entered in the owner's *professio* stayed to work the land. In keeping with former practice, the Roman state could not prevent those who did not own land from leaving it. For this reason it had recourse to a new measure: *coloni* had to remain on the land,

---

duas auri libras ie cogatur exsolvere cuius agros transfuga cultore vacaverit, ita ut eundem cum omni peculio suo et agnatione restituat. Fine to the fisc: C.J.XI 48,12, C.J.XI, 48,52 and C.J.XI 53,1: *Maneatque eos poena qui alienum et incognitum recipiendum esse duxerint, tam in redhibitione operarum et damni, quod locis quae deseruerant factum est, quam multae, cuius modum in auctoritate iudicis collocamus.* See about it ch. *Adscripticii.*

17. A. Cerati, *Caractère annonaire et assiette de l'impôt foncièr au Bas-Empire,* (1975), 283.

18. C.J XI 52,1.

not because of tax, but because of unfulfilled obligations towards the estate proprietor. The right of the possessor to retain an indebted *colonus* was explicitly formulated for the first time in Constantine's law of 332 A.D.[19]; the provision was repeated in later laws.[20] The last region where this rule was applied was Palaestina. The law on Palaestinian *coloni*, C.J.XI 51,1, of 393, is not an act introducing a dependent colonate into this province, as it is thought,[21] but one conferring on owners the right to retain *coloni* and return fugitives: *Sancimus ut etiam per Palaestinas nullus omnino colonorum suo iure velut vagus ac liber exsultet, sed exemplo aliarum provinciarum ita domino fundi teneatur, ut sine poena suscipientis non possit abscendere; addito eo, ut possessionis domino revocandi eius plena tribuatur auctoritas.*

As with other similar laws, the category of *coloni* envisaged by the law is aimed are the indebted, those who had become *coloni iuris alieni*. *Liberi*, i.e. *liberi coloni*, could, like other *plebei*, leave the land they cultivated as tenants, provided they had met their obligations towards the owner.

There are basically two measures that prevented the *coloni* from leaving the *dominus* and the land: the granting of the right to the *dominus* to retain them and the penalizing of the person who gave them shelter: he who sheltered another's *colonus* had to reimburse the tax *(capitatio)* due for the time that had elapsed and also to pay a fine. The penalizing of persons sheltering another's debtor who was liable for tax, is older than Diocletian. A recently published papyrological text dating from the time of Carcalla,[22] shows earlier traces of this practice. A certain Serenus who, seeking that one Herakleides should be returned to him, points out in his application to the state authorities that the fugitive was an ὑπόφορος *(tributarius)*, most likely one who was working on another's land and should have paid poll tax. Serenus then refers to the emperor's edict from the time of Severus, according to which any person concealing another's ὑπόφορος had to pay a fine of 50.000 sesterces. The text does not mention the relationship of Serenus to Herakleidos; Serenus very likely deliberately concealed it, as it would seem that the rule stressed in the edict of Ti.Iulius Alexander was still in force: that the Roman state might only intervene when tax debts were at stake. Since Heracleidos

---

19. C.Th. V 17, 1.

20. C.J.XI 48,8; XI 51,1; XI 52; XI 53.

21. Jones, *Colonate*, 297 and "Capitatio and Iugatio," *JRS* 47 (1957): 88ff.

22. J.D. Thomas, *JEA* 61 (1975): 201ff. (P.Oxy. 3364).

was a *tributarius* who had left the *idia* and gone into hiding elsewhere, ἐπὶ ξένη, the person sheltering him had to be punished and he himself had to be returned, which was the aim of the plaintiff.

There can be no doubt that tax in the provinces even before Diocletian led to a prohibition on abandoning the land. All those who owned it were obliged to return, at least for the *census*, if they had gone elsewhere. There is no information however which would show that the provincial population regarded tax as a factor capable of diminishing anyone's personal freedom. When Cicero speaks of the Sicilian population who worked on the *ager publicus* he calls them *coloni et aratores populi Romani*.[23] Free barbarians who sought to settle on Roman territory in the second, third and fourth centuries, willingly agreed to pay taxes to the Roman state, thus equating themselves with the provincial population. As for those who had arrived on Roman territory as prisoners of war, the status of a *colonus* who paid tax as an *adscripticius* was undoubtedly more advantageous than that of *dediticii*.[24]

There are no data from both the Principate and the Later Roman Empire, which show that tax was regarded as a factor endangering individual freedom. When peasants in the Thracian villages of Skaptopara and Greseitos at the time of the emperor Gordianus threatened to leave the land, this was not because of taxation, but because of abuse and violence on the part of soldiers from a neighboring military encampment. The time when they lived peacefully and prosperously on the land, paying abundant taxes and everything else required, is described in this letter to the emperor as idyllic.[25] They point out, however, that although payment of tax is not their reason for quitting the land, this will nonetheless threaten the fiscal interests of the Roman state.[26]

Taxation was not regarded as a factor which could reduce anyone to a position of dependence. During the Later Roman Empire, when taxation had undoubtedly become an oppressive burden for those who worked either their own or another's land, it was still not seen as diminishing personal freedom. There is evidence that even those who did not pay taxes in person but through another, consid-

---

23. Cic. *In Verr*. II 3, 120.

24. See the ch. "Barbarians on the Roman territory."

25. Dittenberger, *Syll. 888* = Mihailov. IGBR IV 2236, A.D. 238.

26. See line 85ff.: Ἐὰν τε Βαρω[μεθα φε]υξόμεθα ἀπὸ τῶν οἰκείων καὶ μεγίστην ζημίαν τὸ ταμεῖον περιβληθήσεται.

ered themselves   freemen. One of those is in P.Ross.Georg.III 8
(fourth century): the inhabitants of a village address a certain Neho
whom they call δεσότης καὶ πάτρων and κύριος through whom
they have been paying tax from year to year for a long time. Nevertheless, they point out that this has not made them dependent on him,
just as they were not dependent on his father.[27] Other evidence may
be found in Anastasius' law and later in Justinian's, where *coloni* have
retained the right to dispose of their *peculium*, although paying tax
through the *dominus fundi*, are called free, *liberi coloni*.[28]

The core of Diocletian's fiscal reform could be said to lie not in
tying to the land those who worked on it. This had been happening
earlier with the peregrine population in the provinces—the function-
ing of the taxation system cannot be otherwise imagined. Resentment
and negative response elicited another measure: the obligation to pay
poll tax was extended to include Roman citizens. Lactantius, *De mort.
pers.* c. 23, offers clear evidence of this: *Quae veteres adversus victos iure
belli fecerant et ille* (sc.Maximianus Galerius) *adversus Romanos
Romanisque subiectos facere ausus est, quia parentes eius censui subiugati
fuerant, quem Traianus Daciis assidue rebellantibus poenae gratia victor
imposuit.* What had once been a punishment for the vanquished had
now been imposed on Roman citizens. The result of the new *census*
was that all had to pay *capitatio: Post hoc pecuniae pro capitibus
pendebantur et merces pro vita dabatur.*[29] This illustration of the *census*,
imbued with rhetoric and filled with the author's protest, was still
only that of the usual procedure in such circumstances: the land was
measured, the crops grown on it declared, cattle counted and a *census*
of people between the ages of fourteen and sixty taken.

The right granted to the landowner to return a fugitive *colonus*
or to retain by force those planning escape, probably did not initially
apply in Italy, as Constantine' s law of 332, the oldest of this kind, was
intended for the provinces, *ad provinciales*. As may be seen from the
law on the Palaestinian *coloni*, it too was not applied simultaneously
in all the provinces.[30]

---

27. See the line 7ff.: Γινόσκιν σε θελώμεν, Κύριε ἡμῶν Νέχαι, ὅτι οὐδαὶ ἐπὶ
τοῦ πατρὸς σοῦ οὐδὲ ἐπει τῆς εὐπυίας σοῦ τὸ σόμα δεδωκάμεν ἀλλὰ ὁς
ἡνιαύσιος ποιούμεν τὸ ἐ[ν]τάγιον παρέχομεν οὐδεναί.-For ἐντάγιον,   see
Preisigke,*Wörterbuch*, s.v.: *Lieferungauftrag; privater Zahlungsauftrag; Steuererhebungsauftrag.*

28. C.J XI 48,19 (Anastasius); C.J.XI 48,23 (Justinian).

29. Cf . also *Epit. de Caes.* 39, 31: *Parti Italiae invectum tributum.*

30. C.J.XI 51,1: *Cum per alias provincias lex a maioribus constituta.*

TAX AND SOCIAL MOBILITY: HOMOLOGI

The effect of fiscal obligation on the restriction of the right to leave the land by all those who worked on it, in the Early as in the Later Empire, may be examined from the example provided by a group known in Egypt as *homologi*. The term is one of the few confirmed by papyrological evidence of the first, second and third centuries and again in a later Roman law. In modern studies it is mostly interpreted as one of the terms applied to dependent *coloni* in the fifth century. In fact, the text of the law in the Theodosian Code seems to confirm that the *homologi* referred to the rural population, those who, working on their own land and paying taxes directly, were thereby tied to the village in which they were registered in the tax-rolls and those who, as lessees on another's land, were tied to the landowner and through him entered in the tax-rolls.

The discussion on the meaning of the term *homologi*, based on the fifth century law, C.Th.XI 24,6 (A.D.415) has its history. This law is in fact the only testimony about this category of population in the Codes and the only document of this kind dating to the Later Roman Empire. It is on the strength of this law that modern studies classify *homologi* as dependent *coloni*. It is also believed to be the earliest evidence of an established system of dependent *coloni* in Egypt.[1] It is true that papyrological texts of the first-third centuries attest on more than one occasion that the term ὁμόλογος was in use even before

---

1. M. Gelzer, "Studien zur byzantinischen Verwaltung Ägyptens," *Leipziger hist. Abhandlungen* XIII (1909): 77: "Dass man bis 415 in Ägypten nur homologi kante, ist mir ein deutlicher Beweis für die Richtigkeit meiner Austellung am Anfang des Kapitels. Die Voraussetzungen für einen Hörigenstand existieren in Ägypten erst seit 415." He criticizes Waszynski (*Die Bodenpacht. Agrargeschichtliche Papyrusstudien,* (1905), and his opinion that "Homologi *coloni* wurden sie genannt im Gegenstaz zu den anderen, den *coloni adscripticii* die deinen Vertrag mehr abgeschlossen hatten und immer an die Scholle des Herrn gebunden waren." For the different opinions about *homologi*, see B.A. van Groningen, "ʿΟμόλογος ," *Mnemosyne* 50 (1922): 124ff. For the main discussion, see further; cf. also Clair Preaux, "Le servage," *Recueil de la Société Jean Bodin.* 59: "Colons liés par contract"; Günter, *Klio* 49 (1967): 267: "liberi coloni"; A.H.M. Jones, *LRE* II 776: (for the law of 415 A.D.): "The possession envisaged appear to be estates which had been built up out of village lands by outside landlords and were cultivated by their tenants, who, however, remained on the register of the villages—this is perhaps the meaning of *homologi*—and were legally liable to share in their obligations to the state"; Carrié, *Atti* XVII Pap.Congr. 941: "On peut retablir la continuité et l'identité d'un concept juridique et de la realité correspondente à travers la succession de ces trois denominations differentes: *coloni originales, homologi, enapografoi georgoi.*"

Diocletian, but it is explained that its meaning was then exactly opposite to that in the law of 415 A.D. It is supposed that *homologi* at that time were free rather than dependent peasants.[2]

The specific subject of C.Th. XI 24,6 are not the *homologi* but rather the *possessiones sub patrocinio:*

> *Impp. Honor(ius) et Theod(osius) AA.Aureliano p.p.Valerii, Theodori et Tharsacii examinatio conticiscat, illis dumtaxat sub Augustaliano iudicio pulsandis qui ex Caesarii et Attici consulatu possessiones sub patrocinio possidere coeperunt. Quos tamen omnes functionibus publicis obsecundare censemus, ut patronorum nomen extinctum penitus iudicetur.*

This is followed by a passage about *homologi coloni:*

> *Possessiones autem athuc in suo statu constitutae penes priores possessores residebunt, si pro antiquitate census functiones publicas et liturgos quos homologi coloni preastare noscuntur, pro rata sunt absque dubio cognituri. Metrocomiae vero in publico iure et integro perdurabunt, nec quisquam eas vel aliquid in his possidere temptaverit, nisi qui ante consulatum praefinitum coeperit procul dubio possidere exceptis convicanis, quibus pensitanda pro fortunae condicione negare non possunt. Et quicumque in ipsis vicis terrulas contra morem fertiles possederunt, pro rata possessionis suae glebam inutilem et conlationem eius et munera recusent.*

Procedure is also specified in case of desertion from the land: it is the crucial passage about *homologi:*

> *II sane qui vicis quibus adscribti sunt derelictis et qui homologi more gentilicio nuncupantur, ad alios seu vicos seu dominos transierunt, ad sedem desolati ruris constructis detentoribus redire cogantur, qui si exsequenda protraxerint ad functiones eorum teneantur obnoxii et dominis restituant quae pro his exsolutis constiterit. Et in eorum metrocomiarum locum, quas temporis labsus vel destituit vel viribus vacuavit, ex florentibus aliae subrogentur.*

The paragraphs which follow refer to the land abandoned or transferred to others by *curiales* to the church estates in Constantino-

---

2. Preisigke, *Wörterbuch*, s.v. Ὁμόλογος and ibid., *Fachworter*, p.134: Ὁμόλογοι (vgl. δεδειτίκιοι): " die von den Römern unterworfene und Kopfsteuerpflichtige Bevölkerung, daher wohl = *dediticii* = λαογραφούμενοι." See Wilcken, *Ostraka*, ad n.64; Gelzer, op. cit., in n.1,76.

ple and Alexandria and lastly to the tax liabilities of the clergy.[3]

In his *Studien zur byzantinischen Verwaltung Ägyptens*, in 1909, M. Gelzer devotes several pages and his full attention to the interpretation of the law of 415, C.Th.XI 24,6, focusing primarily on the question of *patrocinium*. He believes that in A.D. 415 the Roman state undertook to solve the problem in a new manner recognizing *patrocinium* as an accomplished fact: patrons became *possessores* and, in return, were subjected to taxation. Insofar as *coloni* are concerned, Gelzer identifies two groups of them in the document: a) those who are *vicis adcsripti* and b) those who are *homologi*. The latter terms might apply to Egypt only and mean the same thing as ἐναπόγραφοι. Originally, however, as already noted Wilcken, *Ostraka* I, p.254, *homologi* were free tenants. In this law, on the other hand, they figure as dependent *coloni* bound to the patron by contract. Such contracts Gelzer identifies in three more cases: according to him, the first is the law of 468, C.J.XI 54,1, contesting the legal validity of these contracts: *si quis post hanc nostri numinis sanctionem in fraudem circumscriptionemque piblicae functionis ad patrocinium cuiuscumque confugerit id quod huius rei gratia geritur sub praetextu donationis vel venditionis seu conductionis aut cuiuslibet alterius contractus, nullam habeat firmitatem;* the second, he believes, is to be found in Libanius, Or.XVII, 4-10, when he speaks about "large villages" as they were called, with many owners: Κῶμαι μεγάλαι πολλῶν ἑκάστη δεσποτῶν. See also c. 11 τῶν ἀγρῶν οἱ πολλῶν εἰσὶ τῶν ἐχόντων ἑκάστου μέρος οὐ πολὺ κεκτήμενων. The patron is defined as ὁ τῶν μισθὸν εἰληφώς. The third case is in Gelzer's opinion, a reference to these contracts in Salvian's *De guh.dei* V 8,39-44. The key passage assumed to prove that enslavement was based on a contract on *patrocinium* is the following:

> *nec tamen grave hoc aut indignum arbitrarer, immo potius gratularer hanc potentium magnitudinem, quibus se pauperes dedunt, si patrocinia ista non venderant, si quod se dicunt humiles defensare, humanitati tribuerent non cupiditati. Venditor nihil tradit et totum accipit; emptor nihil accipit et totum penitus amittit cumque omnis ferme contractus hoc in se habeat... etc., inauditum*

---

3. C.Th.XI 24,6,6: *Quidquid autem in tempus usque dispositionis habitae a viro inlustri decessore sublimitatis tuae ecclesiae venerabiles, id est Constantinopolitana atque Alexandrina possedisse deteguntur, id pro intuitu religionis ad his praecipimus firmiter retineri, sub ea videlicet sorte, ut in futurum functiones omnes quas metrocomiae debent et publici vici pro antiquae capitationis professione debent sciant procul dubio subeundas...ete.* For an English translation see Cl. Pfarr, *The Theodosian Code and Novels and the Sirmonidian Constitutions*, New York 1952. He translates *homologi* by "*coloni* who are admittedly liable to taxation."

*hoc commercii genus est. · Cum possessio ab his recessit, capitatio
non recedit: proprietatibus carent et vectigalibus obruunt.*

Gelzer believes that Salvian's text shows how such sham
contracts on *patrocinium* deprived tenants of their freedom. The
situation in Gallia was therefore presumably the same as in Egypt:
unable to pay the tax, *homologi* came under the patronage of *potentes*
thereby losing their freedom by tacit consent. The price they paid was
more than just the μισθός mentioned by Libanius. They relinquished
to the patron their holdings as well while continuing to cultivate them
as tenants. They paid the ἐκφόριον and in return the patron protected them from public taxes and other exactions, but they were no
longer free because they had forfeited both the right to their status
and to *ius libertatis* or, as Salvian says, *ut extorres non facultatis tantum, sed etiam condicionis suae atque exulantes non a rebus tantum suis,
sed etiam a se ipsis ac perdentes secum omnia sua et rerum proprietate
carent et ius libertatis amittant.*

Gelzer takes the year of the law making reference to *homologi*
A.D.415, as the year when the dependent *coloni* first appeared in
Egypt. He does not discuss papyrological evidence since it is of the
earlier date when ὁμόλογος had, as he believes, an altogether
different meaning.[4]

However, other theories trace *homologi* back to papyri and their
commentators. C.Wessely, who does not dwell specifically on this
question, concludes briefly in his commentary of P.Brit.Mus. II 261,
pp.9 sq.:

Sie stehen unter den ὄντες ἐν ὁμολ(όγοις) λαογρ(αφία).
Diese Angabe entspricht unserer Ansicht uber die Bedeutung des
t.t. ὁμόλογος vgl.Wiener Sitzungb. 142,9,25, als die Bezeich-
nung von Ortsfremden Personen die hier ihren Aufenthalt ge-
nommen haben und der Kopfsteuerpflicht sich unterwarfen.[5]

He based his conclusion on the following text of P.Brit.Mus.
261,11.142-143: καὶ τῶι (πρότῳ) (ἔτει) Οὐεσπασιανοῦ ἀπὸ
ξέ(νων) κα[...] σὺν τοῖς πατράσι ἐν ὁμολ(όγοις) ἀνειλ(ημμένοι).
This conclusion is contested by Wilcken. He made his first brief
reference to *homologi* in the commentary in *Ostraka I*,[6] developing it

---

4. Gelzer, op. cit., in n.1, p.74ff.

5. C. Wessely, *Studien zur Palaeography und Papyruskunde* I, 64, line 142.

6. Wilcken, *Ostraka*, published many texts from the 60s of the first century, nos.404-
420. As typical could be treated the n.413, (A.D. 63): ψεναμοῦνις Πεκύσιας
φεννήσιος (sic) ὁμολ(όγῳ) Πιβούχι Πατεήσιος χ(αίρειν) Ἀπέχω παρὰ σοῦ

later into a theory which Rostowzew included in his famous study of the Roman colonate.[7] Wilcken's basic idea is briefly outlined in the above-mentioned commentary in *Ostraka*. Rejecting the link between ὁμόλογος and *professio*, indicated by Zacharia von Lingenthal[8] and, in a certain sense, Zulueta,[9] he goes back to Gothofredus' commentary of the quoted passage in C.Th.Xl 24,6: ὁμόλογοι, *condicionales, dediticii qui videlic.sese dedentes ex pactione quadam hanc in condicionem venerant et recepti fuerant.*[10] They would therefore be persons whose condition derives from a contract, ὁμόλογια, and it would equally apply to the *homologi* of the Early Empire and those mentioned in the Code. Their common feature is that they work on the land and that they do it on a contractual basis. Since the contents of the contract are not known, the substance of the relationship and the *homologi* condition present an insoluble problem.[11]

Slightly a decade later Wilcken was basically still of the same view, except that now he documented it better.[12] He found his crucial evidence in papyri, P.Lond.II 36 and BGU II 560. On the P.Lond II n.259, p.38, the text in ll.63-65 is discussed:

Ἤχθησαν εἰς ἀπαίτ(ησιν) τῷ ιγ (ἔτει) ὁμό(λογοι) ἄνδ(ρες) χ κϑ
ὑπὲρ ι γ (ἔτους) (ἔτων) ξα   ε
[τε]τελ (ευτηκότες) ιγ (ἔτει)   β   ἄνδ(ρες) χλς

Wilcken's thesis rests on the figures attached to some categories in the text and the following arithmetic: if one accepts his reading of χ κϑ in 1.63 of the quoted document there is a total of 629 men; if this is added five persons over 60 years of age, i.e. those relieved of taxes and

---

ςδ ὀβολ(ὸν) τὴν λογίαν Ἴσιδος περὶ τῶν δημοσίων Ꝉ ἐνάτου Νέωνπος τού κυρίου Μεσσορὴ ια. See Wilcken's commentary on p. 254, note 1.

7. Rostowzew, *Kolonatus*, p. 219ff. and *Addenda*, p. 403ff.

8. Zacharia von Lingenthal, *Geschichte des griechisch-römischen Rechts*, 1892³ (1955) 227, note 734: "Homologi heissen sie, weil sie in den Professionen, beim census abgegeben werden mussten." In Günter's opinion, *Klio* 49 (1967): 207, *homologi* were free *coloni* in Egypt.

9. Zulueta, *De patrociniis vicorum*, in Vinogradoff's *Oxford Studies in Economic History* (1909).

10. See his general definition, C.Th. Ad XI 24,6: "Homologos quosdam colonos fuisse in vicis. De his tris hoc l. indicantur: primo, fuisse eos colonorum genus; secundo, ita nuncupatos more gentilicio; tertio, fuisse adscriptos vicis seu dominis, Ex quibus omnibus patet, fuisse colonos adscripticios vicis et fundis adscriptos; denique, colonos condicionales de quibus ago prolixe ad leg.2 infr. De censu."

11. Preisigke, *Wörterbich;* Wilcken, *Chrestomatie*, and n.64

12. Wilcken, in Rostowzew's *Kolonatus*, 221.

two deceased, one gets the sum total of 636 in 1. 65. From this arithmetical operation it is inferred that ὁμόλογοι are the same as λαοραφούμενοι, i.e., the taxpayers.

Wilcken tested his conclusion on BGU 560 = W.Chr.64, ll.20-23 (second century), with his improvement of the text:

.. ..].γεωργοῦντες ὁμόλογοι ἄνδ(ρες)   ρμδ
...]οι (?) γεωργ[οῦ]ντ[ε]ς δημοσίαν καὶ οὐσιακὴν γῆν ἄνδ(ρες) ριε
..]ὁμόλογοι? ἄ]νδ(ρες) ρα ὑπερ(ετεῖς) ιγ ἐνσινῆς   α
..]ε περὶ τὴν κώμην βασιλικὴν γῆς διὰ δημοσίω(ν)

Here are also figures standing next to γεωργοῦντες ὁμόλογοι - 144, those who are γεωργοῦτες δημοσιαν καὶ οὐσιακὴν γῆν 115, those over 60 years—13 and invalid—1. Number 115 is, according to him, a total of 13 persons paying the tax no longer, 1 invalid and 101 *homologi*; the number 144 in the l. 20 Wilcken was unable to account for in his arithmetic.

Having established the link between *homologi* and the tax, Wilcken confronted the problem of ὁμολογῶν λαογραφία, a term attested in many documents: P.Oxy III 478, of A.D.132, in which a freed woman, Dionysia, requests that her son, having attained 13 years of age, be included on the lists of those paying a tax of 12 drachmae, because his father was μητροπολείτης δωεκαδράχμος δι' ὁμολόγου λαογραφίας in the thirteenth year of Hadrian's reign and Dionysia's patroness was also in the class of the δωδεκαδράχμοι . Wilcken holds that this document is about λαογραφία τῶν ὁμολογῶν and refers to the text in *Stud.Pal.I* p.71,1.459 which address adult men only: ἀνδρῶν τε[λεί]ων ὄντων ἐν ὁμολ(όγοις) λαογ(ραφία) ὀνό(ματα) ε καὶ τ[ὰ λο]ιπ(α) ὀνό(ματα) ι. This should then be yet another corroboration of his basic idea that ὁμόλογοι and *dediticii* were one and the same; ὁμόλογος λαογραφία would then be the *dediticii* tax, *dediticische Kopfsteuer*.[13]

Wilcken takes note of two more documents, BGU II 618 and P.Lond.II 259. In the l.13 of the first he reads, after revision of the text, Ἀ]π(ὸ) μὲν ὁμο(λόγου) λαογραφία ἄνδρες δ' ὧν τὸ κατ' ἄνδρα; in the l.9 of this papyrus there is a list of those resident there temporarily to work, as he believes, on imperial domain, like μετατιθέμενοι on P.Lond.III, p.150, καὶ τῶν ἐκ προτροπῆς πρὸς καιρὸν πα[ρὰ] γειν[ο]μένων πρὸς τὴν τῆς γῆς [ὑ]περεσίαν ἄνδρες ξ. Secondly, he discovers the same division into *homologi* and those from the neighboring village in P.Lond.II, p.226 (A.D.133-134): one category are ὁμόλογοι from the village Κερκ(...) and the other

---

13. Wilcken, op. cit., 221.

comprises persons from the neighboring village, καὶ τῶν ἀπὸ Καρ-(ανίδος).[14]

The analysis of these papyri makes Wilcken draw his chief inference: the *homologi* are those who pay the poll-tax *(Kopfsteuerpflichtige)* in their village, on their *idia*, as opposed to those who figure on the lists of land workers originating from neighboring villages and temporarily resident there.[15] This inference runs counter to Wessely's which is based on information supplied by P.Brit.Mus. 261, 1.142 f. σὺν τοῖς πατράσι ἐν ὁμολόγοις ἀνειλ(ημένοι).[16] Here is the reference to those returned from abroad; this should lend further support to Wilcken's conclusion that *homologi* were those entered on tax-rolls on their own *idia*.

Wilcken persists in his view that there is no difference between *homologi* and *deditici* but offers nothing more to support it than Gothofredus who refers to the meaning given this word by Herodotus and Thucydides.[17] He rejects the assumption that *homologi* on BGU 560, as well in C.Th.XI 24,6 constitute a separate social stratum *(bestimmte Schicht)* while granting that the term could have had, in addition to the general, yet another, more specific meaning, covering all the tax payers, that is all persons aged between 14 and 60 and enrolled on their *idia*. As regards the interpretation of the text in C.Th. cit., Wilcken agrees with those who do not distinguish two classes here; *homologi* are, in his opinion, all the *vicis adscripti*.

Wilcken's principal thesis, that *homologi* and *dediticii* are one and the same, is questioned by the editors of P.Ryl.209, J.M.Johnson, V. Martin and A. Hunt. The document they edited and comment speaks of γῆ ὁμόλογος. In this, as in two other papyri, BGU 84 and P.Leipz.105 = W.Chr.237 (I-II century A.D.) it is opposed to another category of land, called ἄβροχος. It was Mitteis who held that ὁμόλογος γῆ was land subjected to taxation as against ἄβροχος γῆ, that is dry, non-irrigated land. To Wilcken, the former is the land its

---

14. Ibid., 222.

15. Ibid., 220f.; Grundzüge, 59-60: "Die Richtigkeit einstweilen vorausgesetzt, es sind die 'ομόλογοι(= dediticii) die gesamte kopfsteuerpflichtige Bevölkerung Ägyptens, einschliesslich der Frauen und Kinder. In diesem weiteren Sinne ist das Wort angewendet in Stud. Pal. I S.64, 142 wo es in einer Liste der ἀφέλικες υἱοὶ λαογραφούμενοι heisst: καὶ τωι (πρώτῳ) (ἔτει) Οὐεσπασιανοῦ ἀπὸ ξέ(νων) κατ-[εἰσελθόντες] o.a. σὺν τοῖς πατράσι ἐν ὁμολ(όγοις) ἀνειλ(ημένοι) κτλ . Hier werden die unter 14 Jahren alten, also noch nicht Kopfsteuer zahlenden Söhne die mit Vatern aus der Fremde heimkert waren doch schon unter die 'ομόλογοι aufgenommen."

16. Ibid., 226.

17. Gothofredus, loc. cit. (See note 10).

owner recognizes as being in a normal, expected condition, i.e. regularly irrigated. To continue upholding the view that *homologi* were for all practical purposes *dediticii*, means to accept that the term ὁμόλογος signified one thing when applied to land and another when applied to people. In their commentary to P.Ryl. 209, ad l. 10, the editors express the view that this link between ὁμόλογοι and ὁμόλογος γῆ need not be given up. Their interpretation of the word ὁμόλογος is based on the meaning it would have if applied to land. It is evident that in the text they edited ὁμόλογος γῆ is opposed to another category of land called ἄβροχος. Since the latter is dry and irregularly watered, the former ought to be land in a regular state regarding irrigation and cultivation hence subject to taxation: "It is clear that ὁμόλογος applied to land means undisputed, tacitly agreed upon, or in a technical sense" concerning which no fresh return has been sent in " and consequently, from the fiscal point of view, liable to its normal taxation." At the same time they admit that this is not the original nor the full meaning of the word.[18] As applied to people, the term ὁμόλογος would mean persons indusputably sub-jected to the poll-tax and not asking to be relieved of it: the conclusion is that ὁμόλογος in P. Brit. *cit.* are those persons who agreed to their liability to the poll-tax and did no ask to be relieved."

The editors of P.Ryl. 209 contest Wilcken's identification of *homologi* as *dediticii*, supporting this with an important counter-argument: if there is no difference between *homologi* and *dediticii*, it is impossible to explain why the group does not comprise those over 60 and the invalid mentioned on P.Brit. Mus. *cit.* Why should one cease to be a *dediticius* upon reaching 60 or because he is disabled?

* * *

Most modern researchers agree that the term ὁμόλογος should be linked with ὁμολογεῖν and that the meaning is "to agree, con-sent, make an agreement." However, even though such an interpre-tation is possible, it need not be the only one. In point of fact, the verb ὁμολογεῖν is confirmed on many documents on loan or lease, the so-called *paramone* texts wherein one party agrees to all, often very hard terms. They are nonetheless agreements between two

---

18. See P.Ryl. 209, p. 287: "It is thus clear that ʹὁμόλογοι applied to land means liable to its normal taxation, though this meaning is not the original one and does not express the full sense of ὁμολγος." In Wilcken's opinion (*Ostraka* I, 254) the meaning of the ʹὁμόλογος originally was just opposite to the latter; they were, as Gelzer (*Studien* 76) formulated it, "Leute deren Stellung auf einer ʹὁμόλογια, einem Vertrag basiert."

individuals, one of whom is much worse off economically and thus forced sometimes to offer his freedom as security that he will fulfill the contract.[19] Such instances do not provide a real analogy with the meaning attached to the ὁμόλογοι in the above-mentioned documents. The main difficulty in accepting the intepretation of ὁμόλογος as "undisputed, tacitly agreed" derives doubtlessly from the fact that the tax, whether levied on land or on the people, could not be the subject of either a contract or an agreement since it was assessed and levied by the Roman state.

If one gives up the attempt to link ὁμόλογος with ὁμόλογία and ὁμόλογεῖν, then one could perhaps try to find some other interpretation, for instance, along the lines indicated by Zulueta in his *De patrociniis vicorum.* [20]He is inclined to look for some association with the words ὁμοδούλος and ὁμοκήνσος assuming that they mean that *homologi* were equally responsible to the state and to the fisc. The root would be the word ὅμος meaning *same, the same, one and the same* as evidenced by many compound words.[21] Two terms, ὁμοδούλος and ὁμοκήνσος are found in passages in *Novella Iustiniani*,128, c.VII and c.VIII, and refer to land, in both cases in relation to *epibolé* and tax liability. In c.VII it is specified as of what moment the one receiving the land indicated as ὁμοδούλος and ὁμοκήνσος and without a master, begins to pay the tax on it: c.VIII specifies when and how are this *epibolé* or *adiectio* done:

Εἰ πότε δὲ συμβαίη δεσπότην οἰασδήποτε κτήσεως ἢ μὴ φαίνεσθαι ἢ πρὸς τὴν τῶν δημοσίων καταβολὴν μὴ ἀρκεῖν, ὥστε διὰ τοῦτο τὴν τῆς ἐπιβολῆς ἀνάγκην γενέσθαι, κελεύομεν παραχρῆμα ταύτην παραδίδοσθαι τοῖς ὁμόδουλα ἢ ὁμόκηνσα χωρία κεκτημένοις μετὰ πάντων τῶν ἐν αὐτῇ εὑρισκομένων γεωργῶν καὶ πεκουλίων αὐτῶν καὶ ἐνθηκῶν καὶ καρπῶν καὶ ζῴων καὶ παντὸς ἄλλου instructou καὶ instrumentοῦ ἐκεῖσε εὑρισκομένου.[22]

---

19. See the Wilcken, *Ostraka,* loc. cit. Cf.Preisigke, *Wörterbuch,* s.v. Ὁμόλογος , 2)

20. Zulueta, op. cit, p. 52, links this to *homologos,* meaning "liable along with the rest of the group."

21. Liddle, Scott, Jones, McKenzie, *Greek-English Lexicon,* s.v. ὅμος.

22. See Latin translation: Si vero aliquando contigerit dominum cuiuscumque possessionis aut non apparere aut ad fiscalium solutionem non sufficere, ut ex hoc superindictionis necessitas suscipiatur, iubemus repente hanc tradi his qui conserva aut contributaria praedia possident cum omnibus qui in ea inveniantur agricolis et peculiis eorum et enthicis et fructibus et animalibus et omni alio instructo instrumentoque ibi invento. For ὁμόδουλος cf. Preisigke, *Wörterbuch,* s.v.: "mitdienend, gemeinsammeer Zwangpflicht oder Haltung unterliegend."

It is evident that in both cases it is the land which has been entered on tax rolls under certain conditions and subjected to same kind of taxation. If it remained without an owner or the owner was unable to pay the appropiate tax, it would be transferred as *epibolé (adiectio)* to those already owning this kind of land, with everything that is necessary to go on with its cultivation, i.e. with γεωργοί and their *peculia*, capital, fruits of the land, livestock, equipment and implements. There is no corresponding Latin terms for ὁμοδούλος and ὁμοκήνσος and the legislator uses in the parallel Latin text a literal translation, *conserva aut contributaria preadia*, relating them both to *fiscalium solutio* i.e. the tax payment. Fiscally speaking, both categories, ὁμοδούλα and ὁμοκήνσα χωρία linked by an *or* are treated equally and it seems quite logical to assume that it was the land where there was labor and that is therefore, from the taxation point of view, equal and equally tax liable. In that case the word λόγος would mean tax.

It is highly noteworthy that in *Novella Iustiniani* cit. both terms mean land where there was labor force available. It is denoted by one and the same term γεωργός, with the broader meaning land worker. Ὁμόδουλα χωρία could be the land worked not only by slaves but by other dependent persons. In this case γεωργός or *agricola* could mean serf and dependent *colonus,* this without *peculium*, the *colonus iuris* alieni. Γεωργός on the ὁμοκήνσα χωρία could mean free peasants as well as *liberi coloni,* those still disposing of their *peculium.* In both cases regardless of whether the land was worked by free or by dependent *coloni,* the taxes was paid through the *dominus fundi.*

The least acceptable part of Wilcken's interpretation is obviously his identification of *homologi* with former *dediticii*. It is contradicted, as it has already been noted, by texts quoted by Wilcken himself and therefore needs to be rejected. On the other hand, the second part of Wilcken's theory, that *homologi* are all those liable for *capitatio* on their *idia* has a firm basis in facts in Egyptian documents and could hardly be disputed. First, that they were those liable for poll-tax seems to be proven beyond'doubt by the fact that the above-mentioned lists of persons specify those over 60 years hence relieved from taxation and the invalids as not accounted as *homologi*. This can be added to the testimony provided by P.Ross. Georg.V 20, of A.D. 223, where a *census* of persons together with those who were ἐκτὸς ὁμολ. is mentioned in line 5. The text's editor explains in his commentary that ἐκτός ὁμόλογοι were those absent from their *idia* at the time. This explanation might hold water if it were not two difficulties: first, the following line begins with those under age, ἀφήλικες, who lived in the same village, i.e. in their homeland , during the emperor Alexander Severus. If we link ἀφήλικες with ἐκτός ὁμόλογου they could be minors not tax-liable yet and therefore not *homologi* either.[23] Secondly, as can be seen in the beginning of the document and in line 4, this text also contains the list of Korfoty villagers and inhabitants of other villages. Ὁμολογο[ι] in line 9 were presumably those from the village Korfoty and registered on the tax-rolls there. Even those who were temporarily absent from the village at the time, remained *homologi*. Those temporarily away from their *idia* were defined on papyrological documents as οἱ πρὸς καιρόν here, to work the land, as in BGU 618 or in papyrus SB 5223, where a specific mention is made of those transferred from town to imperial domain to cultivate them and those entered on village tax-rolls and working tax-liable land: καὶ τοῦ γεωργοῦντος βασιλικὴν γῆν ἀπὸ τῆς μητ[ροπόλεως] πρὸς καιρὸν τῆς γεωργίας παρεμδημοῦντος εἰς τ[ὴν] κώμην πρὸς τὴν τῆς γῆς ὑπηρεσίαν.

If line 7, speaking of ὁμολόγου τας γραφίας τῆς κώμης (villages' *census* related to taxation?) were interpreted as a continuation of the preceding line mentioning προσοδική γῆ, a link between the two terms could be established. This however, gives rise to a new problem: the meaning of γῆ προσοδική. In this particular case it can be left aside; only the basic meaning is important, that it was the taxable land.[24]

Ὁμόλογος was doubtlessly a local Egyptian term for the rural population which was taxed and enrolled in the tax-rolls on their *idia*. They could also have been freeholders and lessees, indebted or free. It seems that the term also meant this in the Later Roman Empire, although it had disappeared from official use after the time of Severian dynasty, probably supplanted in the laws by one of the numerous terms of the imperial chancellory, as for instance *adscripticius*, ἐναπόραφος , *originarius*, etc. and in everyday life by the generic

---

23. Pap. Ross. Georg. V 20, recto (A.D.223): Κορφότυ καὶ [...]Αὐρηλιω Ηραιω τω και Α[ρ]τεμωνι βασ[ς γρς?]παρα μηλ Ηρα[κ]κειδου και Σενασεως των [....]κωμς Κ[ο]ρφοτυ και αλλ κῶ, κατ ανδρα λαογπας συν τοις εκτος ομολ. υφ...[..] αφελικ του δι[ελ α]ς Μαρκου Αυρηλιου Σεουηρου Αλεξανδρου Καισαρο[ς ... κτλ. R. Taubenschlag, in his *Law of Greco-Roman Egypt in the Light of the Papyri*, (1955), p. 594, note, 45, gives the following interpretation: Οἱ ἐκτὸς ᾽ομόλογοι may mean *dediticii*, who in this period were "outside," outside what? The most natural supposition is outside the civitas. If this is correct, the phrase ἐκτὸς ᾽ομόλογοι denotes κωμῆται, villages."

24. Ὁμόλογοι τῆς κώμης in this document does not refer either to οὐσιακή or δημοσία γῆ. In Papyrus BGU 560 numbers indicating people working on this kind of land are not entered in the total number of *homologi* given at the end of the column.

γεωργός, commonly used in the hellenophone countries to denote various categories of the rural population.

After all this a question arises as to whether a link can be established between *homologi* mentioned in early papyrological texts and the Later Roman law of 415 A.D. If one takes as a starting point Wilcken's definition that *homologi* were those paying the poll-tax in their *idia*, then his inference that they are the same ones as *qui vicis adscripti sunt* in C.Th.V 24, 6 sounds logical. But Wilcken, like many other scholars, considers that *homologi* here are *coloni* whether they were tied to a village or to the landowner.[25] He claims also that those who see in the text two different classes, the *homologi* and those *vicis adscripti* are in error.[26]

There does not seem to be a convincing reason to believe that C.Th.cit. is a special law on *coloni*. It speaks of *homologi* in general, i.e. of those liable for *capitatio* and as such figuring on the village tax-records. That is how the wording *vicis adscripti* should be interpreted because in this case they are not the same as *adscripticii*. *Homologi* could be *coloni* as well as small freeholders. As in previous centuries, the tax-payers were not allowed to leave the land they tilled. If they did, they were considered fugitives who were to be returned. In the well-known edict of A.D.154, the prefect Sempronius Liberalis calls those who left the land and wandered abroad "bad *homologi*"; he demands that they be brought back and handed over to him not as suspects, but as those who have not fulfilled their fiscal duties.[27] Similarly, the law of A.D.415 stipulated that fugitives are to be returned. In the case of those who were dependent, the tax due for the time elapsed is to be paid by those who received them.

Basically, Early Empire *homologi*, like those after Diocletian, were tied to their place of birth and to the land by fiscal obligation which could not throw doubt on their status as freemen. But all

---

25. Wilcken, bei Rostowzew, Kolonatus, 226.

26. Wilcken thought that *homologi* were all *coloni,* but rejects as ill-documented the opinion that there were two groups of *coloni,* one named *homologi* and another who were *vicis adscripti.* In this critique he probably had in mind Gelzer and his theory, *Studien,* 75: "Es handelt sich um zwei Arten von Bauern: 1.*Vicis adscripti,* 2. *homologi.* Die einen begeben sich *ad alios vicos,* die anderen *ad alios dominos.*" Gelzer himself rejects Waszynski's interpretation that this law reflects two groups, *coloni homologi* and *coloni adscripticii.*

27. BGU II, 372, ll. 20-25 = W.Chr. 19: Ἐ[ὰ]ν δὲ τὶς με[ ] τὰ τὴν τοσαύτην μοῦ φιλανθ [ρ] ωπίαν ἐ [π]ὶ ξένης ϸλανώμενος φανῇ οὗτος οὐκετιὼς ὑποπτος ἀλλὰ ὡς ὁμόλογος κακοῦργος σ [υ] νλημφϸεις πρὸς μὲ ἀναπεμφ[ϸῆσε] ται. See Wilcken's commentary in *Chr.* Ad n.19: would δenote a brigand (*Verbrecher*). See also van Groningen, op. cit, 128, note 1: "Sunt enim confessi scelerati nefarii certi, quos ipse facta notent."

homologi, freeholders or dependent *coloni* alike, found themselves in an identical position concerning one matter: tax liability restricted their freedom and prevented them from leaving the village where they had been put on tax-rolls.

DEBTS AND FREEDOM:
SLAVERY BY CONTRACT

The status of homologi in Egypt exemplifies how taxes reduced, if not personal freedom, at least the opportunity of leaving the land for various categories of the rural population. During the Principate this applied mainly to peasant freeholders who had their own farms and during the Later Empire to free peasants and *coloni,* if the latter were dependent on the landowner, *dominus terrae.*[1]

Dependence of the *colonus* on the land possessor was the result of indebtedness and unpaid rental arrears and did not disappear even in those cases where the poll-tax (*capitatio*) was abolished. Telling proof of this is to be found in the law on the *coloni Illyriciani,* C.J.XI 52: when the *capitatio* was abolished, the *coloni* could not leave the land they had cultivated and go where they wished because it was not the tax that bound them to the land, but their status as *coloni: inserviant terris non tributario nexu, sed nomine et titulo colonorum.* The lease contract could bind the *colonus* to a certain estate and to his owner. The *colonus* did not fulfill the conditions of the lease, he was in debt because he had not paid the rent due. Indebtedness of those who worked on land that did not belong to them is an occurrence common to all ancient societies as it was in other ages.[2] Some ancient states, such as Egypt and Athens, enacted laws forbidding enslavement for debts. Among the Romans *nexum,* the harshest form of enslavement, was prohibited by *lex Poetelia* in the early Republic. However, in Rome, Italy and the provinces by pre-Roman tradition, indebtedness could lead to a reduction of the debtor's personal freedom. Even after Poetelius debtors were rigorously treated, so that a praetor or other magistrate could permit the creditor *addictio* (the "leading away") of the debtor.[3] This measure led to a temporary

---

1. The link between the tax burden and flight of peasants from land in Egypt I have recently discussed in *Flucht der Bauern, Fiskal und Privatschulden,* Studien zur Geschichte der römischen Spätantike, Festgabe für Professor Johannes Straub (1989) 147ff.

2. I.M. Finley devoted one of his most persuasive papers to this topic, "Debt bondage and the Problem of Slavery," *Revue d' histoire de droit français et etranger* 43(1969) = "Economy and society in Ancient Greece," 34ff. , with many examples from various societies in theAncient World. Lin Foxhall in *JRS,* 80 (1990) 97ff. addesseses the problem of tenancy, using a sociological methodology, and drawing not always well chosen parallels with today's Third World.

3. For the *nexus* problem see M. Kaser, *Privatrecht* 148ff. .with bibliography. This is briefly summarized by M.N. Frederiksen, in "Caesar, Cicero and the Problem of Debt," *JRS* 56 (1966):129ff. For *obaerati,* see the short article in *RE* XVI I 2 (1937)

restriction on the debtor's freedom, probably until he worked off his
debts. For a *colonus* working off rental arrears that increased from
year to year, this restriction could last a long time, even for life, and
arrears could pass on to his descendants. In Roman Egypt, a lease
contract or a debt was guaranteed in the person of the contractor or
members of his family, though enslavement for debts had been
abolished as early as the eighth century B.C.[4]

The sources contain much information on the restriction or loss
of freedom due to debt in the Roman state after Poetelius' law, for
example Liv.XXIII 14,2 (212 B.C) or Sall., *In Cat.*33 (letter from the
supporters of Catilina);[5] the most important for the problem of
dependent *coloni* are data in Varro's *Res rustica* and in the Columella's work: Varro, RR I, 17:

> *Omnes agri coluntur hominibus servis aut liberis aut utrisque;*
> *liberis, aut cum ipsi colunt, ut plerique pauperculi cum sua*
> *progenie, aut mercennariis, cum conducticiis liberorum operis res*
> *maiores, ut vindemiae ac faenisicia, administrant, iique quos*
> *obaerarios nostri vocitarunt et etiam nunc sunt in Asia atque*
> *Aegypto et in Illyrico complures.*
>
> Columella RR I 3,12: *Tantum enim obtinendum est, quanto est*
> *opus, ut emisse videamur quo potiremus, non quo oneraremur ipsi*
> *atque aliis fruendum eripuimus more praepotentium qui possident*
> *fines gentium quos ne circumire quoque valent, sed proculcandos*
> *pecudibus et vastandos ac populandos feris derelinquunt aut*
> *occupatos nexu civium et ergastulis tenent.*

The *obaerati* (Varro) and *nexus civium* (Columella) are worthy
of note. Varro himself in LL I 7,107 describes *obaerati* as debtors
working off their debts: *liber qui suas operas in servitutem pro pecunia*
quam debeat dat, dum solveret, nexus vocatur, ut ab aere obaeratus. It is
thought, however, that they no longer existed in Rome or Italy at the
time of Varro, but only in the provinces Asia, Egypt and Illyricum.
This is not an indisputable conclusion emerging from Varro's text in
RR. In fact, he does not claim there are no more in Italy, but that
there are some *now* in the provinces he names: "Those which our
people call *obaerati*, and there are some now in Asia, Egypt and

---

col. 1692 (Dull).For Varro's data, see recently D.Flach, *Römische Agrargeschichte*,
in Müller's *Handbuch* III-9, (1990), 157f.

4. For *paramoné*-contracts, see O.Montevecchi, *I contrati di lavoro e di servizio nell'*
Egitto greco-romano e bizantino, (1950), 5ff. and B.Adams, *Paramone und verwandte*
Texte, Studien zum Dienstvertrag im Rechte der Papyri, (1964), especially pp.45ff.

5. See Frederiksen, op. cit.

Illyricum."[6] *Nunc* alone in the sentence following this in which the
obaerati are named is insufficient to conclude that they at one time
existed in Italy. Debtors of this type, working off debts with a
temporary loss of freedom, existed even at the time of Columella.
They were probably those whose land *(peculium* in Later Roman
sources) passed into the possession of creditors as a *pignus* for unpaid
debts or rental arrears and who fell into temporary slavery. Large
estates also consisted, according to Columella, of land taken from
others–*aliis fruendi eriperimus,* he says in the same sentence. It should
not be forgotten that this author also mentions *ergastulum* on which
work enslaved citizens. It is usually thought that this was a workshop
for slaves. But this meaning does not fit into the context of *nexus
civium. Ergastula* must have been workshops intended for slaves, in
which free citizens *(cives)* worked to pay off debts. In this sense it is to
be found among other authors,[7] including Livy at one point, in II 2,6:
ductum se ab creditore non in servitium, sed in ergastulum. He obviously had in mind the time following Poetelius' law which mitigated
the original harshness toward debtors and prevented real enslavement
for debt. The possibility remained, however, for creditors to use the
labor of the debtor until the debt was worked off. It could be said that
this retained its importance in the centuries after Poetelius.

It might be said that both Varro and Columella speak of an
occurrence which Dio Chrysostom in his *Discourse on Slavery and
Freedom* , XV 23, calls "slavery by contract": Ὅτι μυρίοι δήπου
ἀποδίδονται ἑαυτοὺς ἐλεύθεροι ὄντες ὥστε δουλεύειν κατὰ
συγγραφὴν ἐνίοτε ἐπ' οὐδένι τῶν μετρίων ἀλλ' ἐπὶ πᾶσι τοῖς
χαλεπωτάτοις.[8]

This is also contained in numerous documents from Egypt,
known as *paramoné*-contracts, according to which anyone taking a

---

6. See Finley, op. cit., in n.2: "When we called *obaerati* (or *obaerarii*) and who still
exist in large numbers in Asia, Egypt and Illyria." P. Garsey, "Non Slave Labour in
the Roman World," *Proceedings Cambr. Philol. Society,* Supp. 6 (1980): 47, n. 11, poses
the question whether we may assume that Varro in his account excludes the Italy of
his own time, when he says that *obaerati* now exist in Asia Minor and Illyricum. The
answer is affirmative, in support of which he cites Brunt's opinion.

7. For instance Caes.*BC* III 22,2: Svet.*Tib.*8: *HA, Vita Hadr.* 18. For *ergastulum* see
Oxford Latin Dictionary,s.v. "A kind of prison on a large estate to which refractory
or unreliable slaves were sent for work in chain-gangs." Cf. German translation,
K.Ahren, *Columella über Landwirtschaft,*1986,57: "Schuldgefangene und Straflinge,"
or English translation, H.B.Ash, ed.Loeb Class. Library, p.51: "Possessings...occupied
by citizens enslaved for debts and by chain-gangs."

8. "Thousands and thousands of people, albeit free, deliver themselves up by contract
to others in slavery to work not under moderate conditions, but in the worst possible
circumstances." Trans. By T. W. Cohoon, Loeb Clas. Texts II, 1977, p. 164.

lease or loan of land undertook, in the event of his not fulfilling the terms of the contract, was forced to place himself and all he possessed at the disposal of the creditor. The following document, P.Oxy.499 of A.D.121 may be quoted as typical of this group of texts:

> Tryphon son of Aristandrus and Sarapion son of Herodes, inhabitants of Oxyrhynchus, have leased to Apollonius son of Horus of the village of Senepta, Persian of the Epigone, for the present sixth year of Hadrianus Caesar the lord from their property at the said village in the holding of Dion the ten-and-a half arourae upon which corn has been grown, of which the adjacent areas are on the east the land of Didymus, on the south that of the aforesaid lessors, on the north the same, on the west the land of Seuthes son of Potamon, which land is to be cultivated with grass for cutting and grazing at the rent for each aroura, without a survey being made, of 36 drachmae of silver, guaranteed against all risk, the taxes upon the land being paid by the lessor, who shall be the owner of the crop until he recovers the rent. If this lease is guaranteed, the lessee shall pay the rent in the month Pauni of the said year and shall forfeit any arrears increased by one half and the lessor shall have the right of execution upon the said Apollonius and upon all his property as if in accordance with a legal decision.

There are also *paramoné*—documents referring to the temporary enslavement of the debtor's children: the debtor would give his son to remain night and day in the creditor's house, to carry out certain tasks until the interest on the debt was paid off. Following this he was free again, like the *addictus* and not emancipated as in the case of a slave.[9]

The restriction of the freedom of people who were free by origin due to debt was widespread in many countries before they became part of the Roman state. This continued into the Roman period. There is much evidence, among the most eloquent are the following examples:

Cic. *Pro Flacco*, 20,48, quotes the example of Herakleides of Temnum, who was handed to his fellow-citizen Hernippus as an *addictus* by the Roman provincial authorities, as he could not pay back a debt. Hernippus was given the right to take him away: *cum iudicium non faceret, addictus Hernippo et hoc ductus est.*

Plutarch in *De vitando aere alieno 4*, draws attention to the dangers of mortgage and debt; the only way out for debtors was often to seek asylum in the shrine of Freedom:

---

9. See Adams, op. cit. in n. 4, p.17 f., and for example P.Flor. I 44 (A.D.158) or P.Nessana 56 (A.D.687) - the latter is found outside Egypt.

ἡμεῖς δὲ τὴν αὐτάρκειαν αἰσχυνόμενοι καταδουλοῦς μὲν
ἑαυτοὺς ὑποθήκαις καὶ συμβολαίοις δέον εἰς αὐτὰ τὰ
χρήσιμα συσταλέντας καὶ συσπειραθέντας ἐκ τῶν
ἀχρήστων καὶ περιττῶν κατακοπέντων ἢ πραθέντων
ἐλευθερίας αὐτοῖς ἱερὸν ἱδρύσασθαι καὶ τέκνοις καὶ
γυναιξίν.[10]

There is some evidence of this in the Celtic and German
countries. Caesar in BG VI 13 speaking of two classes in Gaul, says:
The common people are by position at the level of slaves, either
pressed by debt, enormous taxes or injustice of the powerful who had
the same rights as a slave owner: *Plerique, cum aut aere alieno aut
magnitudine tributorum aut iniuria potentiorum premuntur, sese in
servitutem dicant nobilibus: quibus in hos eodem sunt iura que dominis
in servos.* In another passage, BG I 4, Caesar mentions *obaerati* of the
Helvetian leader Orgenorix: *Die constituta causae dictionis Orgetorix
ad iudicium omnem suam familiam, ad hominum milia decem, undique
coegit et omnes clientes obaeratosque suos, quorum magnum numerum
habebat, eodem conduxit. Obaerati* are also mentioned by Tacitus with
the tribe of Treveri, speaking of the rebellion of Florus, Ann.III 42:
Aliud vulgus obaeratorum et clientium arma cepit.

Provisions affecting *addicti* were kept in some provincial laws.
One from Gaul, *Lex Rubria de Gallia Cisalpina*, FIRA I p. 97, c.XXII,
provides *addictio* for those who do not pay back debts or do not
respond to a court summons: *eosque duci bona eorum possideri
proscribeive iubeto.* A similar regulation may be found in the *Lex
Ursonensis* in Spain, FIRA I, p.12, c.XXI: *Ni vindicem dabit iudici-
umque faciat secum ducito.*

Some traces of the original severity towards debtors remained in
the Roman state throughout the centuries. There is evidence of this
in the Late Empire also. Ambrosius' *Liber Singularis de Nabathe* gives
a dramatic description of the leading away of a debtor: *Vidi ego
pauperemduci dum cogeretur solvere, quod non habeat, trahi ad carcerem
quia vinum deerat ad mensam potentis, ducere in auctionem filios suos,
ut ad tempus poenam differe possit.* The selling or pledging of children
in the case of debts was a widespread practice in the Late Roman
Empire and Diocletian enacted two laws in an attempt to prevent it.[11]

---

10. See an English translation by H.N.Fowler, Plutarch's *Moralia*, Loeb class.
Library, vol. X, (1969), 321: "But we, ashamed to be independent, enslave ourselves
by mortgages and notes, when we ought to limit and restrict ourselves to actual
necessities and from the proceeds of the breaking up or the sale of useless super-
fluities to found a sanctuary of Liberty for ourselves, our children and our wives."

11. C.J.IV 10,12: *Ob aes alienum servire liberos creditoribus iura compelli non
patiunturi;* VIII 16,6: *Qui filios vestros vel liberos homines pro pecunia quam vobis*

Colonus rental arrears might have been one of the ways to indebtedness—one which led to a real restriction of freedom. Many years before Diocletian the relation of the *colonus* to the *dominus fundi* was no longer that of a free peasant to the landowner. At the end of the Republic the *coloni*, along with slaves and those who had been emancipated, are found in the suites of powerful men. [12] Tacitus in a passage from *Germania*, c.25, describing slaves among the Germans, compares them with the *coloni* in reference to their duties toward the landlords: *suam quisque sedem, suos penates regit, frumenti modum dominis aut pecoris aut vestis ut colono iniungit et servus hactenus paret: cetera domus officia uxor ac liberi exequuntur.*

Indebtedness of the *colonus* due to rental arrears, a familiar occurrence by the end of the Roman Republic, must have become widespread during the crisis of the Later Empire. The Roman state could have responded as did the Athenian at the time of Solon or the Egyptian in the eighth century, by legally prohibiting the rendering of freemen dependent on those to whom they were in debt. In the distant past, there had been Lex Poetelia, forbidding *nexus* in the Roman state. However, it did nothing of the sort. Admitting that the *coloni* were practically in the position of slaves, sixth-century laws speak of the *nexus colonarius*. In spite of that, the legislator continues to insist that the *colonus* is still free. His dependence on the proprietor of the land, brought about through debt and rental arrears, was used by the state for fiscal reasons. The *colonus* of the Later Empire, a man who had no land, in theory could not be taxed within a system which took man as work force (*caput*) and land (*iugum*) together as a fiscal unit. He worked another's land. The Roman state also gave the right to the landowner, as the *dominus* to whom the *colonus* owned rent, to keep him on his estate as a private debtor.

In the time of Pliny, the payment of accumulated rental arrears had become impossible; we do not know if the *coloni* on Pliny's estate were able to leave the land before paying their arrears; but the departure of a *colonus* of the Later Empire from the land he tilled remained only a theoretical possibility. The dependence of the *colonus* was in fact dependence of the *dominus fundi* and is to be found as the definition of *colonus* given by St. Augustine, *De Civ.Dei.*X 1,2: *Appelantur coloni qui condicionem debent genitali solo propter agricul-*

---

credebat pignoris titulo accepit, dissimulatione iuris se circumvenit, cum sit manifestum obligationem pignoris non consistere nisi in his, quae quis de bonis suis facit obnoxia (A.D.293).

12. See Caes. B.C. I 34: *Profectum item Domitium ad occupandam Massiliam navibus actariis septem quas Igilii et in Cosano a privatis coactas servis, libertis, colonis suis compleverat;* Salust., Cat. 59, 3: *Ipse (sc. Marius) cum libertis et colonis.*

turam sub dominio possessorum, and left traces in the *Tabletes Albertini* from Vandal Africa: *Particulae agrorum ex culturis suis mancianis sub dominio Fl. Gemini Catullini flaminis perpetui.*

    Colonus as a title undoubtedly meant a man of certain social status even in sources dating from the Later Republic or Principate. It was a man who worked on another's land not having any of his own. In the Later Empire and frequently in legal texts this term is a synonym for a dependent lessee, someone who because of the overdue rent can no longer leave the estate on which he works. Any realistic chance of repayment by working for the landowner disappeared. Besides indebted *coloni,* however, there were also those who were independent, who had either their own land or other property which was freely at their disposal. The difference between both categories of *coloni* lingered into the Later Empire. It was emphasized in certain laws, mainly those referring to the return of fugitives to the land they worked. After Diocletian there were both *liberi* and dependent *coloni.* Only the latter were tied to the landowner, had to work on his estate and to pay off arrears of rent, which in some cases had accumulated throughout several generations. The laws refer to these by the term *coloni iuris alieni.* As a category they merit special attention in discussion of the freedom of the *coloni.*

COLONI IURIS ALIENI:
INDEBTED AND ENSLAVED

The earliest mention of *colonus iuris alieni* is in the famous law of Constantine, issued in 332 A.D., C.Th.V 17,1:

> *Imp. Constantinus A. ad provinciales. Apud quemcumque colonus iuris alieni fuerit inventus, is non solum eundem origini suae restituat, verum super eodem capitationem temporis agnoscat. Ipsos etiam colonos, qui fugam meditantur, in servilem conditionem ferro ligari conveniet, ut officia quae liberis congruunt, merito servilis condemnationis compellantur implere.* Dat. III Kal. Novemb. Pacatione et Hilarione conss.

This is added to the *Interpretatio* of the fifth century: *Si quis alienum colonum sciens in domo sua retinuerit, ipsum prius domino restituat et tributa eius quamdiu apud eum fuerit, cogatur exsolvere: ipse vero qui noluit esse quod natus est, in servitium redigatur.*

We find mention of the same category of *coloni* in later texts, in the law of Gratianus, Valentinianus and Theodosius, C.Th.V 17,2 *(colonus iuris alieni)*, in all probability in C.J.XI 48,8 *(profugi qui alieni esse videtur)* and in C.J.XL 52,1 *(alienus colonus)*, issued in the seventh and ninth decade of the fourth century. Some regulations in the laws concerning Illyrian and Palaestinian *coloni*, in C.J.XI 53,1, A.D.371 and C.J.XI 51,1, A.D.393(?) probably refer to the same group styled *alieni coloni* or *coloni iuris alieni* in previous laws.

The law of Constantine, C.Th. V 17,1 was the crucial text in discussions concerning the dependent colonate—considered in all histories of the Later Roman Empire and in many studies with a direct or indirect bearing upon colonate as the first unambiguous evidence about the existence of the bound colonate. The provision of this law is generalized and its application is made broader to include all *coloni* and the entire agricultural population.[1] *Colonus'* attachment

---

1. E. Stein, *Histoire du Bas-Empire* I, 1968,17, with the remark in the note 6 that the law of Constantine of 332 was not the imperial constitution that bound the *colonus* to the soil in most of the provinces (see also Kornemann, RE Suppl.IV,1924,92; O. Seeck, *RE* IV 1901,489, s.v. *Colonatus*), but rather that this *régime* was introduced earlier on by Diocletian's fiscal reform. A. Piganiol, *Empire chrétien*,1972 [2], 306 presumes the existence of an earlier law that would have bound the *colonus* to his *origo*. In his opinion the origin of this practice can be found in the fiscal policy of the third century. However, in some of the modern studies the possibility of small peasants being dependent and bound in the provinces, in some cases even in pre-Roman times, is not denied (M. Rostowzew, *Kolonatus*, for example). But recently R. McMullen in the book *Roman Government's Response to Crisis A.D.235-337*

is primarily considered due to his fiscal obligation and interpreted as the consequence of the fiscal policy of the emperors of the fourth century.[2] In that regard a *colonus* would be no different from the rest of the agrarian population. That a penalty would be imposed only on the *colonus* in the case of desertion is explained by the fact that the free peasants who owned their land did not run away. The relationship between *colonus* and landlord is considered of little importance in the process of tying *colonus* to the land he cultivated.[3]

The authors of some recent papers, investigating the development of the colonate during the early centuries of the Empire also take as their point of departure the belief that the reign of Diocletian brought about major changes. A *colonus* of the Later Empire would be quite different from the one living in an earlier period. During the early centuries of the Empire he was a free man who could conclude a land-lease contract and leave the land he was cultivating even if he had failed to pay his rent in time; he was entered in the tax-rolls and paid the tax in his own right. On the contrary, in the fourth century and later, a *colonus* is tied to the land he farms and pays the tax

(1976):179 maintains that the Roman government did not try to immobilize the rural population through legal measures before Constantine, he being the first to do so with his own *coloni*. For a systematic review of theories of the origin of the Later Roman colonate, see Clausing, *Colonate* and M. Kaser, *Das römische Privatrecht II.Abschnitt*,1975,[2] 142-143, note 5. For bibliography see ch. Foreword.

2. According to Palasse, *Orient et Occident*, 17, the struggle for binding *coloni* to the land started at the time of Diocletian's fiscal reform: if *coloni* of the third century were already dependent, then that dependency was legally defined by the fiscal innovation of the Later Empire. For A.H.M. Jones, *Colonate*, 1ff. the loss of a *colonus's* freedom was the consequence of the imperial legislation in Diocletian's time. (see idem, *LRE*, 796: "The liberty of tenants was probably first restricted byi the census of Diocletian ... by the legislation which, for fiscal motives, tied the peasantry to their place of registration, where they paid their *capitatio* and *annona*." Segrè, *Colonat*, 103ff. and Goffart, *Caput and colonate* 71ff. consider binding of *coloni* to the soil to be a consequence of imperial legislation in the seventh and ninth decades of the fourth century. For a similar view, see also Saumagne, *L'origo* 486ff, in particular 494ff.

3. Although Fustel de Coulanges, *Le colonat*, 83 sees the formation of the colonate as a process that considerably predates Diocletian, he nevertheless comes to the conclusion that the government began to show interest in the colonate for fiscal motives; he interprets the law of Constantine of 332 as the emperor's intention of solving the problem of tax payment (p. 89). See the opinion of P. Garnsey, Cambridge Philol. Society, *Proceedings*, 1980, Suppl.6, 39: "In my view, the solution of the notorious problems of the rise of colonate lies in the peculiar conditions of the late third and fourth centuries, in particular the increasingly oppressive tax burden and any attempt to trace a continuous trend from Principate to Late Empire across the great divide of the third century is doomed to failure." The role of *dominus fundi* in the process of loosing the *colonus's* freedom is completely neglected by Jones and Goffart.

through the landowner. From a man who was once free, he becomes a slave of the land, *servus terrae*.[4]

The theory that taxes were the decisive factor in binding the *colonus* to the soil has remained the starting point in some recent studies. The law of Constantine, C.Th.V 17,1, still holds an important place in these discussions, but it is no longer considered to be the document that proves the *colonus* had lost his freedom and the right to leave the estate. Its various interpretations are irrelevant to the problem of determining the date of origin of the dependent *colonus*. This law would not curtail his right to leave land. The legislator's intention was not to prevent a *colonus* from leaving the estate he worked on, but to compel him to perform his fiscal duties in the place where he had been registered on the tax-rolls. The term *colonus iuris alieni* in C.Th.V 17,1 is interpreted as the expression used to denote that the *colonus* was "under contract" or obliged to the landowner, which did not affect his legal position or his status. As a free tenant-farmer he was at liberty to leave when he pleased.[5]

The first law that reflects a change in the situation would be, as it is supposed, that of 361, C.Th.XI,1,7. It rendered senators liable for taxes of their fugitive *coloni* and anticipated by a decade a distinction between two kinds of *coloni*, those who were a part of the landlord's tax declaration (*professio*) and those who paid their own taxes. In the first case, senators were responsible to the government for their *colonus*'s taxes. The process of binding *coloni* to the soil would seem

---

4. W. Held, "Das Ende der progressiven Entwicklung des Colonates," *Klio* 52, (1970): 239ff. supports the view that the position of *coloni* underwent a change toward the end of the second and the beginning of the third century; but in this paper as well as in his book, *Die Vertiefung der allgemeinen Krise im Westen des römischen Reiches*, (1974), he retains the traditional and generally accepted conclusion that it was only in Diocletian's time that the agricultural population was included in the local tax-rolls and bound to the soil.

5. This point is strongly emphasized by W. Goffart, *Caput and Colonate*, 71ff. His interpretation influenced Eibach's study of the Later Roman colonate. Accepting Goffart's main conclusion, Eibach interprets the position of the *colonus* as defined in Constantine's law of 332 A.D. as follows: 1. *coloni* were at this point still free men, the term *ferro ligari* did not refer to their legal status; 2. *coloni* were tied to their origin by fiscal policy and a legal relationship that cannot be more closely defined; 3. the term *origo* is here used in its "classical" sense, as the place of origin where one paid one's tax (Eibach, *Kolonat*, 50 ff, in particular 51: "Auch zur Zeit Konstantins haben wir denoch keinen konkreten Hinweis auf eine durchgängige Anwendung des *origo*-Princips in Richtung auf eine zwangsweise Bodenbindung des Pächters-Kolonen. Erst gut zwei Jahrzente später ist eine solche Tendenz nachweisbar." In a review of Goffart's book, this interpretation of Constantine's law of 332,C.Th.V 17,2 is qualified as "against the natural sense of the passage" (Duncan-Jones, *JRS* 67, (1977),202).

to be under way. Similar tendencies are to be discovered in Valens'
legislation in the East. It also differentiates between landowning
coloni who pay their taxes to the tax-collectors and those who do it
through a landlord or his agents. In Goffart's opinion there are three
parts in the laws of Valens: the amendment of the existing law of 357
had provided that, if the estate was sold, the *coloni* were transferred
along with the land to the new owner (C.Th.XIII 10,3); the law
emphasized the responsibility for hiding fugitive *coloni;* and last of
all, *coloni* no longer exist as citizens who pay taxes. Fiscal liability
was replaced with attachment to the soil. The law concerning *coloni
Illyriciani* of A.D.371 deals already with the *nomen et titulum
colonorum.*[6] Goffart concludes that although the law of 371 did not
institute the bound colonate, it was the first documents that stated the
distinctive characteristics of this institution. This law replaced the
colonus duty to pay *tributum* with the bond to the soil.[7]

All studies on the origin of the bound colonate emphasize two
points: first, those that focus on the continuity in the development
of the colonate, tend to determine a fixed date which would mark the
transition of the free tenant-farmer to the dependent *colonus* of the
Later Roman Empire who is forbidden to leave the land he cultivated;
and second, the principle of binding to the soil is generalized and
communis opinio is that it was applied not only to different categories
of *coloni,* but to the entire agricultural population. Some of the laws
that are the basis of modern theories, however, concern only certain
categories of *coloni* and others clearly differentiate between degrees of
dependency of the various categories. The law of Constantine of 332,
cit., refers to a certain category, the one styled *coloni iuris alini* and
this important proviso must be kept in mind when discussing either
the concrete content of the law or its place and importance in the
formation of the bound colonate.

Three aspects of this question deserve attention: the relation of
the *colonus iuris alieni* to his fiscal obligation; the relationship
between *colonus* and proprietor; the question of the legal position of
this category of *coloni.*

The basis of the theory that the state instrumentally tied the
colonus to the soil lies in the conviction that the *colonus* was a free
man as long as his name appeared on the tax-rolls and he paid the
taxes himself; a change in his legal status was brought about only
when the tax was transferred from the *colonus* to the land, i.e. to the
landowner. The shift of the tax liability from the *colonus* to the

---

6. C.J.XI 53,1

7. Goffart , *Caput and Colonate,* 75f.

dominus fundi was, as it is generally agreed, the basis for converting the hitherto free *colonus* into the slave of the land he cultivated. By making the landlord accountable for the payment of the tax, the state authorized him to coerce the *coloni* into staying on the land.[8]

The fiscal question occurs frequently in the legislation of the Later Roman Empire. In its onesidedness it primarily dealt with the duties of citizens to the government. The principle valid in the laws of the fourth century was that basically the proprietor was liable for the land tax. The law C.Th.XI 1,14 is quite clear on this point.[9]

The principle that ultimately the proprietor was liable for the tax on the part of the estate cultivated by *coloni* is emphasized in the law of A.D.361,C.Th.XI 1,7 which should not be seen as anticipating the state of affairs, but rather as the confirmation of a long standing principle. It specifies in which cases the senator is tax liable for the *colonus* who has fled from the land: *Compertum est pro colonis profugis ad exsolvenda vos fiscalia conveniri. Iubemus igitur, si nihil ex eorundem terris senatorum quemquam possidere constiterit, ut nulla cuiquam pensitandi pro his qui aufugerint necessitas imponatur.*

From this text it is clear that in the case of *colonus'* flight it was senator's duty to pay the tax due only if he was landowner. This law treated senators not as members of the highest class, but as landowners. The *coloni* in question must have been those who, not possessing land of their own, were entered in the *professio* of those whose land they worked, i.e. of senators.

The problem of the *decurio's* tax liability was solved in a similar manner by a considerably earlier law, from 319 A.D, C.Th.XI 7,2: *Unusquisque decurio pro ea portione conveniatur, in qua vel ipse vel colonus vel tributarius eius convenitur et colligit.* According to this law the *decurio's* fiscal duties were those of the landowner and its conclusion emphasizes the principle: *nullus pro alio patiatur iniuriam.* Undoubtedly, as in the case of senators, the tendency and practice existed to render the economically and socially most influential class responsible for the tax on estates which did not belong to them. This was prevented by law.[10]

---

8. Goffart, op. cit., 80.

9. See ch., Tax and Freedom.

10. Earlier studies maintain that this law defined the *decurio* as the owner (Palasse, *Orient et Occident,* 370); A. Cerati, *Caractère annonaire et assiette de l'impôt foncier au Bas-Empire,* (1975),30, n. 60, gives a new interpretation: *tributarius* would here mean "contribuable relevant de la *portio* du territorium ... d'un decurion déterminé." Thus each decurio would be responsible only for his *portio,* "ou lui même, son colon ou le contribuable relevant de lui doit payer l'impôt et juir d'un revenu foncier." The former interpretation, in which a *decurio* appears only as a landowner, seems to

The question of the landowners' fiscal obligation in previous centuries is also of significance in considering the importance that fiscal policy had in the formation of bound colonate. If the independent entry of the *colonus* in the *libri censuales* is to be taken as the essential distinction of a free man, then it follows that some categories, primarily those who did not possess land, lacked this qualification long before the fourth century. One of the regulations in the well known law *De censibus,* preserved in the *Digesta* under the name of Ulpianus, L 15,4, states that the landowner was held responsible for the correct registration of his estate and the manpower on it. In the case of false *professio* he was liable to punishment by imprisonment.[11]

As it has already been noted, the text in *Digesta* brings to mind the Lactantius' description of the *census* conducted by Diocletian, *De mort.pers.*23. It must have concerned among other things, as did the laws dating from the late fourth century, the fiscal liability a landowner bore for the parts of his estate he did not cultivate himself. The principle, that in the situation where the paying of taxes proved difficult, it was ultimately the proprietor who bore the responsibility to the government, must have been an ancient one. Early evidence, which would affirm this practice in the Late Republic and in the Principate is to be found in the provinces. Cicero, for instance, *In Verrem* III 22,53, mentions the case of Xeno from Maenae whom Verres held liable for tax on part of his estate cultivated by a *colonus.*[12]

be more acceptable. In Goffart's opinion (op. cit 82) the *decurio* is protected by this law from the responsibility for the tax on the land pertaining to another *decurio.*

11. Fustel de Coulanges, *Colonat,* 75 concludes that the *colonus* was entered along with the slaves in the tax register of the *dominus fundi.* He interprets the aforementioned passage in the *Digesta,* L 15,4, as follows: the owner was left with the choice of either registering the tenant in the tax-rolls, in which case the tenant paid the tax due or of paying the tax on the land himself regardless of who cultivated it.

12. J. Carcopino, *La loi de Hièron et les Romains,*1924, 206.f. believes the cited text offers enough evidence to conclude that, regardless of who owned the land, it was ultimately the tenant who bore the fiscal responsibility. Judging from the papyrological texts, however, it was mostly the landowner who had to pay taxes to the state (see A.Ch. Johnson, in Tenney Frank, *ESAR* II 77 and 82. Cf. texts of P.Lond. 314 or P.Aur.Isid. 99 and others). Contracts in which the tenant assumed the tax liability were few. But in cases in which difficulties arose in the payment of tax (as for instance flight of *coloni*) the owner of the estate was liable to the government for the tax. For Verres, see M. Gelzer, *RE* VIII A-2,(1959),1603ff. On the basis of Cicero's text in *Verr.*III 22,54, H. Degenkolb, *Die Lex Hieronica und das Pfanderecht,* (1861), 46, had already concluded that the practice of registering estates and the manforce working on them was common practice in the provinces at a date considerably prior to Diocletian. Undoubtedly it was in the landowner's interest to be registered in the tax-rolls with as few *iugera* as possible—compare the grievance of an Egyptian farmer of A.D. 244 that he had been registered in the tax-rolls with more *iugera* than he in fact possessed, P.J. Parsons, *JRS* 57, (1967),134.

But as he had taken flight, it was evidently the proprietor who bore the ultimate fiscal responsibility to the government. There is some link between this case and the legislation of the fourth century. Xeno was responsible for the tax on the land the fugitive *colonus* had been cultivating in the same way as the *decurio* was in accordance with the law of 319 or the *senator* in accordance with the law of 361. It is therefore possible and moreover probable that these two laws, C.Th.XI 1,7 and XI 7,2 are concerned with the enforcement of an already existing general practice, in order to protect decurions and senators who were frequently liable for the tax on land that did not belong to them.

The law of Constantine of 332 does not concern the fiscal liability of a *colonus*. He was not obliged to pay it to the government, as the land he cultivates does not belong to him. The tax due during the time he spent on a certain estate was to be paid by one whose land he cultivated. A. Cerati's interpretation of this law would seem to get the heart of the matter: the *colonus'* person was of fiscal value and together with the other *coloni* was basis for determining the *capitatio* of the land he had left. Deprived of his labor, the *dominus fundi* still paid tax determined by the original estimate, while that same *colonus* at the new estate where he worked represented a value which had not been declared. It was therefore just that compensatory tax be demanded from one who profited from his work.[13] This assumes that the law of 332 refers to *coloni* who were registered on the tax-rolls under the landowner's name. Inevitably one comes to the further conclusion that the *colonus iuris alieni* in question could not have been a free man who paid his taxes and was free to leave his tenancy and farm when he wanted to. The latter is clearly stated in the law: if he is found on another's land, he is to be returned, in all probability to the estate on whose *descriptio* he was originally registered.

The laws of 319 (C.Th.XI 1,7) and 361 (C.Th.XI 7,2) concerned the question of land tax liability in cases where the *colonus* left the land he had been cultivating; the law of 332 C.Th.V 17,1, however had in mind another aspect of the same problem: that of fiscal debts in the case where the *colonus* was found with another landlord. The penalty for concealing fugitive *coloni* corresponds to earlier practice.

13. Cerati, op. cit., in n.10, 283f. Fustel de Coulanges, *Colonat* 89 reasoned in a similar way: the possessor's tax liability to the government for his *colonus* leads one to the conclusion that the new *dominus* according to the law of 332, C.Th.V 17,1, was the one who had to pay the tax for the *colonus* during the time the latter spent on his estate. The same principle would be, in his opinion, applied to the *mancipia* in the law of 327,C.Th.XI 3,2: *sublatis pactionibus eorundem onera ac pensitationes publicae ad eorum sollicitudinem spectent, ad quorum dominium possessiones eaedem migraverunt.*

In the papyrological text cited above from the time of the Severan
dynasty the imperial edict of 200 A.D. which decreed that a person
concealing a ὑπόφορος *(tributarius)* was to be fined 50.000 sesterces
is quoted.[14] Imposing a fine for the concealment of *coloni iuris alieni*
was not uncommon practice even in the legislation of the later fourth
century: the law of 386 decreed that the concealment of a private
colonus iuris alieni would be fined 6 ounces of gold, that who was
patrimonialis— one libre (C.Th.V 17,2)

There is a certain similarity between the law of 332 and the
imperial edict from 200 A.D., referring to the concealment of person
styled ὑπόφορος—this term could be equivalent to *colonus iuris alieni*
in the law of 332. The edict of 200 A.D. decrees a fixed fine for the
concealment of *hypophoros;* Constantine's law envisages the compensatory payment of taxes owed to the government. But these two
documents differ in some aspects from the other edicts issued by
Egyptian prefects in the previous centuries. The latter summon all
those who had left their *idia* and were away from home to return; no
punishment was envisaged for those who did.[15] All of which leads us
to the conclusion that two groups of edicts existed: one, for all agricultural population in the provinces who, probably in order to avoid
fiscal duties, abandoned their farms, two, a penalty for sheltering of
persons who were in a way dependent on those who paid tax on the
land that they had left. It seems that both these cases were included in
a law from the second half of the fourth century, C.Th.X 12,2,3: *Si
quis etiam vel tributarius repperitur vel inquilinus ostenditur, ad eum
protinus redeat cuius se esse profitetur. Nihilo minus etiam eo pergat*

---

14. J.D. Thomas, "A Petition to the Prefect of Egypt and related Imperial Edicts,"
JEA 61,1975,201ff. 'Ὑπόφορος' is a new word in papyrological texts and according
to the *Corpus Glossariorum latinorum* was the Greek equivalent for the Latin
tributarius. Thomas accepts the interpretation given for the latter by A. Segrè,
Traditio 5 (1947):103 f.: "a taxpayer who is bound to the soil" and assumed that the
edict, issued by Severus in 200 A.D. was the first one to render any absence from
one's *idia* illegal. He rightly links this text with Constantine's law of 332 (op. cit.,
217). It was Severus' innovation to punish for concealing a fugitive.

15. Lond. III, 904 = W.Chr. 202; BGU II 372 = W.Chr.19; see the group of documents dating from Severus' time: D.J. Crawford and P.E. Easterling, *JEA* 55,
(1969),188ff. (P.Westm.Coll.3); SB I 4284 = P.Catt.2, of 207 A.D. and P.Gen.16 =
W.Chr. 354 from the same year; P.Flor.I 6 of A.D.210; BGU I 159 = W.Chr.408 of
216 and P.Oxy.3364.Cf. Thomas, op. cit., 212ff. who suggests, p.218 that "it may be
also, as we saw, that in the second edict in our text he (sc. Severus) is attempting to
confine the population of Egypt to the *idia* (i.d.nome) in which each person was
born. Such moves, especially the latter, would have to be seen as foreshadowing
developments that were to become prominent in the period after Diocletian." The
edict of Vibius Maximus by A.H.M. Jones, *Colonate,* 5 was treated as "a foreshadowing of later practice."

indago, ut cuncta rimando cognoscat, utrum is fuerit petitionis hortator, qui iniquae retentionis invidiam aliquo necesse habuerit colorare velamine; ut si colonos eadem occulere arte quaesiverit, indemnitatem sarciat tributorum; si servos, ad eam poenam, quae dudum est legibus constituta, teneatur. Quisquis autem plebeium se adserit esse vel liberum, fide rei ostensa ab omni molestia vindicetur et ad ea loca, ex quibus eum esse claruerit, remittatur.

This law considers two categories: first, non-landowning *coloni* who did not pay tax, this being the landpossessor's responsibility (anyone sheltering fugitive had to take fiscal liability for him); second, those styled *plebei* and *liberi*, probably *liberi coloni*.[16] Anyone receiving them was free of any fiscal obligation, while they were returned to their place of origin. There is no doubt that the latter paid their own taxes. This regulation is in accordance with the law C.Th.XI 1,14 in which the *possessor* of land no matter how small, paid the tax due on it. As some papyrological documents from the fourth decade of the fourth century show, punishment for leaving one's land did not exist.[17] The fugitive, however, was compelled to return to his *origo*.

The legal and other texts mentioned lead us to conclude that tax liability effected the immobility of the agricultural population in the provinces even before Diocletian's fiscal reform. The cited documents from the first three centuries of the Empire—imperial edicts or edicts issued by provincial governors—were concerned with returning those who possessed land but had abandoned it. Severe punishments for those who attempted flight, such as the one usually reserved for

---

16. See C.Th.XI 53,1, A.D.371, according to which, if one received *coloni* of whom it had been said they ... *inserviant terris non tributario nexu, sed nomine et titulo colonorum*, one was held responsible for the damage suffered by the *dominus* of the estate the *colonus* had left and was penalized with a fine; for receiving a fugitive slave, the fine was four times as much in addition to the payment of damage; finally, there is mention of free *coloni: in liberis etiam, quos pari usurpatione susceperit, is modum sit, quem circa liberos diximus colonos retinendum.* Eibach, *Kolonat,* 219ff. believes this text to have concerned two categories of *coloni:* the first comprised those tied to land *tributario nexu,* the second—those who were independent, being *nomine et titulo coloni.* Carrié, *Opus* 2:221 criticizes Eibach for overlooking the fact that slaves could be used as *coloni* as well (*servi quasi coloni*). Therefore he deemed it essential that the editor of the law specify *free coloni* "c'est à dire libres se trouvant dans la situation de colons, s'il voulait que les affranchis fussent tratés comme des libres, et non comme des esclaves." It seems probable that so-called free *coloni* were in a similar position as the landowner, being liable to pay tax in the place where they were registered on the tax-rolls.

17. Cf. C.J.Kramer and N.Lewis, *Trans. and Proc. Amer.Philol.Soc.* 68, (1937), for a papyrus of A.D.340, regarding the case of inheriting daughters who had abandoned land. On their return they succeeded in reclaiming their land, together with the rent due from those who had been cultivating the estate in their absence.

slaves—being put in irons—was applicable only to the category of
coloni who were *iuris alieni*. The law referring only to this group,
C.Th.V 17,1, has become in modern studies the first evidence of the
binding of the entire rural population to the land.

In Constantine's time *coloni iuris alieni* already existed as a
separate category. It appears that the tax was not the primary reason
for their origin.[18]   Between these *coloni* and the Roman state,
regarding the fiscal obligations, the *dominus fundi* or *possessor* is a fact
which must not be left out of consideration.

The position of *coloni* who were *alieni iuris* is designated in
legal texts of the fourth century in the following way: they could not
live as free men, as one who is *suo iure, velut vagus ac liber* (C.J.XI
51,1) or claiming to be free men who are their own master, *quasi sui
arbitri ac liberi* (C.J.XI 48,8) to leave the fields they are cultivating, *ex
his locis quorum fructu relevantur abscendere* (C.J.XI 51,1). If they
should do so and go to another, *si abscesserint ad aliumve transierint,*
they are to be brought back and imprisoned, *revocati vinculis
poenisque subdantur* (C.J.XI 53,1); in case of attempted flight they
may be put in chains, *in servilem conditionem ferro ligari conveniet,* in
order that they must, justly be punished as slaves, perform the duties
that fall to them as free men (C.Th.V 17,1). In accordance with the
relevant laws, in cases where they were found with another landowner, they are to be returned, *ipsum prius domino restituat,* in the
Interpretatio of the C.Th.V 17,1, *origini suae restituat* and *cum omni
peculio suo et agnatione,* as is formulated in the law C.J.XI 52,1.

The government supported and emphasized the landlord's
authority. The law concerning the *coloni* in Thrace, C.J.XI 52,1 con-
ferred the right on the *dominus fundi* to prevent the flight of *coloni:*
*Sed possessor eorum iure utatur et patroni sollicitudine et domini
potestate,* and in a similar way the law on Palaestinian *coloni,* C.J.XI
51,1: *Sancimus, ut etiam per Palaestinas nullus omnino colonorum suo
iure velut vagus ac liber exultet, sed exemplo aliarum provinciarum ita
domino fundi teneatur, ut sine poena suscipientis non possit abscendere;
addito eo, ut possessionis domino revocandi eius plena tribuatur auctoritas.*

The authority of the *dominus fundi* over the *colonus* is a fact

---

18. See Fustel de Coulanges, *Colonat,* 85. The legal texts emphasize that *coloni,*
regardless of whether they were registered independently on the tax-rolls or not,
could be dependent on a certain *dominus fundi,* see C.J.XI 50,2 (C.Th.V 19,2):
*Coloni censibus dumtaxat adscripti, sicuti ab his liberi sunt, quibus eos tributa subiectos
non faciunt, ita his, quibus annuis functionibus et debito conditionis obnoxii sunt, paene
est ut quadam servitute dediti videantur.* Carrié, *Opus* 2,224-225 considers this law to
be clear evidence that the *conditio* of *coloni* had a fiscal basis.

which is taken into account in legal texts in the fourth century; it appears also in literary texts of the Later Roman Empire.[19] There is no evidence about its origin. The laws stating that *coloni* and *inquilini* had to stay on the land that they had once undertaken to cultivate, as it was in accordance with the law of ancestors (*Lex a maioribus constituta*)[20] does not explain the origin of the *colonus'* tie to the land, nor the authority of the proprietor. Basically the relationship between the landowner and the *colonus* was the same as it had been in the time of Principate. It would probably have involved a private tenancy contract.

It is frequently emphasized that *coloni* were free men who could leave the land they cultivated whenever they pleased until the time of Constantine and later. Undoubtedly certain categories of *coloni* could do so in the time of the Later Roman Empire as well, but on condition that they had fulfilled obligations to the possessor undertaken by contract. This could not have been the case with the group styled *coloni iuris alieni* in the fourth-century's laws. The regulation that attempted flight should be punished by imprisonment in chains shows how drastically a colonus' freedom had been restricted. Although by origin unquestionably free men, *coloni* of this category had ended up in a dependent position, most probably through neglecting to fulfill their obligation to the proprietor whose land they worked. The *colonus'* arrears, as it has been stressed in some earlier studies, must have rendered them debt bondsmen.

This practice was not unknown in the first centuries of the Empire and in some provinces had its roots in pre-Roman times. Evidence in some legal and literary sources casts a doubt on the explanation that changes in fiscal policy of Diocletian or one of the emperors of the fourth century transformed free *coloni* to slaves of the land they cultivated. If the origin of the dependent status of *coloni* is regarded as a process that began before Diocletian's time—an idea that was not unknown in earlier historiography and is accepted by some

---

19. See Augustine, *De civ.dei* X 1,2: *Coloni qui conditionem debent genitali solo propter agriculturam;* Salvian, *De gub.dei* V 38-39: *(Pauperi) tradunt se ad tuendum protegendumque maioribus, dediticios se divitum faciunt et quasi in ius eorum dicionemque transcedunt.*

20. C.J.XI 51,1: *Lex a maioribus constituta colonos quodam aeternitatis iure detineat, ita ut illis non liceat ex his locis quorum fructu relevantur abscendere nec ea deserere quae semel colenda susceperunt.* It is difficult to accept that this text refers to a law passed by one of the predecessors of the above-mentioned emperors. The case cited by Libanius, *Or. XVII*, 13 and 17, confirms that the owner's right to keep *coloni* on the land dates from previous centuries: Jewish peasants whom Libanius is charging for abandoning his estate they had worked for four generations, i.e. from the second century. See L. Harmand, *Libanius, Discours sur les patronage,* 1959, 188.

modern historians[21]—then it is easy to understand how important was
the role tenants' arrears.

We find *reliqua colonorum* in legal texts of an earlier date, as well
as in legal texts of Paulus and Papinianus concerning the inheritance
or sale of land.[22] Pliny's frequently quoted Ep.IX 37 offers clear
evidence of this practice:

> *cum me necessitas locandorum praediorum plures annos ordinatura*
> *detineat, in qua mihi nova consilia sumenda sunt, nam priore*
> *lustro, quamquam post magnas remissiones, reliqua creverunt; inde*
> *plerisque nulla iam cura minuendi aeris alieni, quod desperant*
> *posse persolvi; rapiunt etiam consumuntque quod natum est, ut qui*
> *iam putent se non sibi parcere.*[23]

It is clear that the *coloni* in question had worked for Pliny for a long
time and that they were indebted. Tenants' arrears were no longer an
unusual occurrence at this time. Some land possessors compensated
for losses thus caused by selling of *pignora*. Pliny condemned this
practice maintaining that it led to exhausting of *colonus* manforce
who would go on creating *reliqua*;[24] he attempted to solve the problem by replacing monetary rent with a part of the revenue derived
from the land cultivated by the *colonus*.

Frequently exercised right to sell the *colonus' pignora* left many
coloni without property. Once indebted, the *colonus'* chances of
paying his arrears were very small. The debt was increased by interest

---

21. Fustel de Coulanges, *Colonat, passim;* see also W. Held, "Das Ende der progressiven Entwicklung des Kolonats," *Klio* 52 (1970):239ff.; some feature of
dependent position of the *coloni* before Diocletian discovers N. Brockmeyer, "Der
Kolonat bei römischen Juristen der republikanischen und augusteischen Zeit,
Historia 20 (1971):732ff.

22. For *reliqua colonorum* see *Dig.* XXXIII 2,32,7 (Scaevola); XXXII 78,3: 97;
XXXVI 7,46 (Paulus); XXXII 91; L8,5 (Papinianus); XXXIII 7,20,3. Cf. Seeck, *RE*
IV,1901,489, s.v.*Colonatus.* Concerning *colonus'* debts see Cicero, *Epist.ad fam. XIII*
11,1.

23. Pliny's text leaves no doubt that the tenant's arrears in question dated from
previous leases and it would be wrong to speak of *reliqua* as current debts of *coloni*
on the basis of this text (A. Ranovič, Kolonat v rimskim zakonodatelstve II-V vv.,
VDI 1951,1,98). Garnsey, op. cit., in n.3,139 thinks they were left with the option of
leaving. However, the strict application of the regulation of *locatio-conductio* would
mean that the *colonus* was free to leave only on fulfilling his obligation.

24. Pliny. *Ep. III 19: Nam possessor prius saepius vendidit pignora et dum reliqua*
colonorum minuit ad tempus, vires in posterum exhausit, quarum defectione rursus
reliqua creverunt. Fustel de Coulanges emphasized that the substitution of part of
the revenue in place of monetary rent was the crucial moment in the formation of
the dependent colonate (*Colonate*, 37).

and new obligations. Losing property they had pledged as security, many free tenant-farmers found their position equal to those who from the beginning had been landless and who hired out their labor and worked for *merces*. When land could no longer be pledged as security and the *colonus* no longer possessed any, he pledged the harvest from the part of the estate he cultivated and to which he belonged. The landlord owned it until the *colonus* had paid the rent.[25] Thus the *colonus* found himself in the position of being able to pay debts only through his labor. This circumstance affected the obligatory renewal of tenancy which meant the *colonus* was not able to leave the land he cultivated until his *reliqua* had been paid. If the *colonus* died, his heir, even though not a *colonus* himself, had to take on the unfulfilled obligation.[26] As early as the end of the Roman Republic, indebted and impoverished *coloni* who had rent arrears belonged to the lower classes and were seen alongside slaves and freedmen in the escort of powerful men.[27]

The laws of the Early Roman Empire protecting the *coloni* from maltreatment by landlords (unlawful increase of rent, breaking of contract leases prematurely, retention of *colonus* after the expire of leases) cannot be treated as the features which distinguished the early colonate from that of the Later Roman Empire.[28] We find similar regulations in the legislations in the time after Diocletian.[29] The interest of the landowner were also protected by law. If the *colonus*

---

25. Concerning the landowner's right to the entire crop until the tenant's arrears had been paid, compare *Dig.* VII 4,13 (Paulus); concerning the liability of the *colonus* to harvest and sell the crop before payment of arrears, see *Dig.* XIX 2,2,9; Gai *Inst.*IV 147 and C.J.IV 65,5. The same is attested to in the papyrological texts, P.Oxy. 1124 (A.D.26) and 499 (A.D.121).

26. *Dig.* XIX 2,60,1 (Labeo): *Heredem coloni, quamvis colonus non est, nihilo minus domino possidere existimo.* Brockmeyer, *Historia* 20:738, perceives a tendency here to make the tenancy hereditary, or at least to ensure it. It did not expire with the death of a tenant.

27. See Caes. B.C.I 34; Salust., *Catil.* 59,3.

28. C.J.IV 65,11 (Philip the Arab), concerning the prohibition against an increase of the agreed rent; C.J.IV 65,11,16, about premature breaking of contract in the time of Valerianus and Gallienus; C.J.IV 65,11 (A.D.244) against detaining of *colonus* after the expiration of the lease. See Ranovič, op. cit., in n.23, p.87 who stresses that in cases that proved difficult, the law was on landowner's side if difficult to prove on the basis of the legal texts. See also Brockmeyer, op. cit., 741.

29. See for instance C.J.XI 50,1: *Imp. Constantinus A. ad Maximum vicarium Orientis. Quisquis colonus plus a domino exigitur, quam ante consueverat et quam in anterioribus temporibus exactum est, adeat iudicem, cuius primum poterit habere praesentiam et facinus comprobet, ut ille qui convincitur amplius postulare, quam accipere consueverat, hoc facere in posterum prohibeatur, prius reddito, quod superexactione perpetrata noscitur extorsisse.*

was unable to pay the rent specified in the contract, the proprietor of
the land was entitled not only to the crop, but also to the *colonus'*
other property until the rent was duly paid. The *peculium* of the
colonus served as a pledge (*pignus*) and in case of an outstanding debt,
the landowner had the right to sell it.[30] The law protected the
landlord from loss through the destruction of inventory or neglect of
the estate and as early as the Late Republic gave him the right to
represent *coloni* in court in all matters concerning the land.[31] These
legal regulations are rooted in the Roman practice of *locatio-conductio.* A general decline in the economy, as well as the increasing
difficulty in obtaining laborers in the Late Roman times resulted in
more rigorous enforcement of existing laws. There seems to have been
no radical changes.

It seems likely that the practice of the earlier times as well as the
later laws distinguish between *coloni* who, having fulfilled their
obligations to their landlords, could leave freely and cultivate the land
of other landowners and those who were tied either to a certain
landlord or estate. It is only in the second group which comprised
coloni of different origin, that we find those styled *coloni iuris alieni*
of A.D.332, *alieni* in some later laws.

If the aforesaid is correct, then they were by origin free tenant-
farmers who were bound to the landowner as a consequence of
tenants' arrears accumulated over a number of years. They were
obliged to stay on the estate in order to pay off debts with their labor.
It is already clear from Pliny's text that *coloni*, having lost all hope
that they be able to pay debts dating from previous leases, no longer
even made the effort to do so; thus the relationship between *dominus
fundi* and *colonus* developed into one of creditor and debtor. As the
debts were not annulled by death of the landlord, the *colonus*
remained on the estate when it became property of the proprietor's
heir. The status of the indebted *colonus*, like that of other debt-
bondsmen, put them in a category between free men and slaves. They
could not be made slaves, as ancient Roman law prohibited the
enslavement of those who were by origin free born; in practice,
however, debts led to the limitation of freedom in the centuries to
come in the passing of the Lex Poetelia as well. There is evidence from
the later times that confirms it.[32] *Nexus civium* in Columella's work

---

30. See n.24 (Pliny's text) and *Dig.* XLVII 2,8 (*fructus as pignus*), C.J.IV 65,5. See
Kaser, *Privatrecht* I,466.

31. Cf. Brockmeyer, *Historia* 20: 741ff.

32. For *nexum* and the question of debt in the centuries to follow the *Lex Poetelia*,
see U.von Lübtow, ZSS 1950,112ff.; P.A.Brunt, *JRS* 48 (1958):168; M.W. Freder-

can only be understood as meaning temporary loss of freedom through indebtedness. The ancient debt law had lost its original harshness, but it preserved its importance in later centuries. Sources mention the terms *addictus* and ἀγώγιμος, meaning persons who had acquired a dependent status through indebtedness. *Iudicatus* and *auctoratus* would come under the same category of terms. The latter, as Kunkel proved, using a series of examples, doesn't denote a gladiator, as had been believed, but in most cases a person who had become dependent on another through debt.[33]

Although according to Roman law a free citizen could lose neither *status ingenuitatis* nor *status libertatis*, many who were free by birth were in practice in a position closer to slave than free man. In one passage in Quintilianus's *Institutio oratoria*, the question is raised of the difference between *servus* and *addictus*. The difference lies, according to Quintilianus, in that the former, on gaining freedom, became a *libertinus*, while an *addictus* regained the status of a free man.[34] Fortunatianus in the fifth century, discussing the differences between people, classifies slaves and *addicti* in the same category, set apart from the others by their *condicio*.[35]

One of the ways that an *addictus* could regain his freedom was

---

iksen, *JRS* 56 (1966):128ff. Cf. E.Weiss, RE Suppl.VI 1935, 60 f. and M. Kaser, *Privatrecht* I, 148 f. For the right of executing debtors in the provinces, for instance in Egypt, see A.Ch. Johnson, *Economic Studies*, 1949,171ff. and for others, Mitteis, *Reichsrecht, passim.* For Rome and Italy, see, for instance Livy, XXIII 14,3 who cites under the year 212 B.C. the case of a man who was put in chains *(in vinculis)* because of the debts; Sallust, *Cat.*33; Colum.RR I 3, cf. ch. *Debt and Freedom.*

33. For ἀγόγιμος see L. Mitteis, *Grundzüge II*,46 and 121; *addictus: Th.LL,* s.v. *addico,* with many examples about debts. Compare *Dig.* XXXVII 10,13,2 (Ulpian); Gai III 199 *(Iudicati* and *auctorati).* For *auctorati,* as persons dependent on the will of others, usually as a consequence of debts they had to work off, see W. Kunkel, *Auctoratus,* Symbolae Taubenschlag III,207ff.(Eos XLVII,1957). The simple entry of tenant in contract in itself could not change a man's status (cf. D. Nörr, ZSS [1965]: 87ff., who contests De Robertis' thesis in *"Locatio operarum" e "status" del lavoratore,* Studia et documenta historiae et iuris 27,1961,19ff., that it was the hiring of one's labor that put one in the position of subjugation and led to the status' change.)

34. Quint. *Inst.Orat.VII* 3,26: *Circa propria ac differentia magna subtilitas: ut cum quaeritur an addictus quem lex servire, donec solverit, iubet, servus sit? · Altera pars finit ita, servus est qui est iure in servitute; altera qui in servitute est eo iure quo servus, aut, ut antiqui dixerunt, qui servitutem servit...Servus cum manumittitur, fit libertinus, addictus recepta libertate ingenuus.* See C.Th. V 19,2: *Coloni censibus dumtaxat adscripti sicuti ab his liberi sunt, quibus eos tributa subiectos non faciunt, ita his quibus annuis functionibus et debito conditionis obnoxii sunt, paene est ut quadam servitute dediti videantur* (the time of Arcadius and Honorius).

35. Fortunatianus, *Ars rhetor.* 2,1 (21 ways of differentiating people), among others: *conditione ut servus, addictus; conditione alia quae liberos spectat, ut adoptivus, addictus...etc.*

to pay his debts off through his work. Varro's well-known sentence, LL VII 107, *liberi qui suas operas in servitutem pro pecunia quam debebat (dabat) dum solveret nexus vocatur* "A free man who gives his labor in servitude for money which he owes, until he has worked off the debt, is called *nexus*" means that it was possible to compensate debts by work.[36]

The tendency to put a debtbondsman in a semi-dependent position, approaching that of a slave's, was known even before Constantine's time. Laws of Diocletian's reign warned that such a practice was forbidden.[37] It is evident that this practice could not be prevented and the law of Constantine, A.D.332, can be treated as a reflection of the real state of affairs in which the indebted *colonus* became dependent on the *dominus fundi* whose land he was not allowed to leave. The *colonus* who was *iuris alieni* was to perform the duties appropriate to him as a free man (probably meaning that he was to work as a tenant on somebody else's land), but if he attempted to avoid it, he was to be treated as an absconding slave. His work was to replace rent he had not paid.[38] The term *iuris alieni* as used in this and other laws is not in its strictly formal sense—it basically could mean that these *coloni* who did not possess land were bound to work for a specific landlord to whom they were paying back debts created by a tenant's arrears. In the first centuries of the Roman Empire, a landless *colonus* had no right to sell his *peculium* without consent of the landowner, as it represented the *pignus* the landowner could sell to compensate eventual losses if the rent was not paid.[39] Conversely, the proprietor was responsible for all transactions connected with the land, including payment of tax.[40] If we regard *coloni iuris alieni* as debtors—those who were convicted for indebtedness or as those who had to work off their debts—then in some aspects their status

---

36. For this and others cases, see Finley, *Debts-bondage*,159; for working off debts, see von Lübtow, *ZSS* (1950):112ff.

37. C.J. IV 10,12 ; VIII 16,6.

38. C.Th. V 17,1.

39. See Pliny. *Ep.* III 19. For the prohibition against sale of the land belonging to the tenant without the knowledge of the *patronus* in the Later Roman Empire, see C.Th. V 19,1 (A.D.365): *Non dubium est, colonis arva, quae subigunt, usque adeo alienandi ius non esse ut, et si qua propria habeant, inconsultis atque ignorantibus patronis in alteros transferre non liceat.* It seems more likely to have been a question of protecting the landowner from the loss he would suffer if the *colonus* sold land that could serve as *pignus,* rather than the landowner's fear that a *colonus* would sell land of which he was not owner, as Goffart, *Caput and Colonate,* 77, note 34, supposes.

40. See Brockmeyer, *Historia* 20,745f.

resembled that of persons' who were not *sui iuris*. In case of theft, as can be seen from Gaius, *Inst*. III 199, a *colonus* was in the same position as *liberi in potestate* and *uxor in manu*.[41]

The *colonus*' temporary loss of freedom developed into a lasting and in some cases hereditary tie to a landowner and his estate. It may be assumed that the number of *coloni* who were unable to pay or work off their rent arrears even in the Early Empire was not inconsiderable. In centuries when it was not difficult to find tenants, however, indebted *coloni* who tried to avoid their obligations by taking flight were not subject to special laws; but in the worsening economic situation of the third century and later, the practice of leaving the land, primarily of those who were working land that did not belong to them, grew considerably. Constantine tried, as did Severus before him, to prohibit such practice by law. Later centuries also witnessed loss of land through indebtedness by the poor and their compulsion to work for their creditors in return for a negligible part of the harvest. Justinian was one of the emperors who attempted to prevent the harshness of creditors by law.[42] The position of those who were prohibited from leaving the land they cultivated approached that of slaves and a sixth-century law renouncing the illusion of freedom in this case, raises the question: *Quae enim differentia inter servos et adscripticios intellegitur cum uterque in domini sui positus est potestate?*[43]

Fustel de Coulanges developed the theory that indebtedness was the root cause for the existence of the dependent *coloni* in the first centuries of the Roman Empire and earlier. The indebtedness of peasants was not an isolated occurrence in ancient Greek and Roman

---

41. Gai III 199: *Interdum autem etiam liberorum hominum furtum fit, veluti si quis liberorum nostrorum qui in potestate nostra sint, sive etiam uxor quae in manu nostra sit sive etiam iudicatus vel auctoratus meus subreptus fuerit.* According to classical law, *coloni* did not fall in the category under *patria potestas*, Gai IV 153, but the position of those who were indebted must have been considerably different. In some ways their status resembled that of persons who were not *sui iuris*, as for instance in the disposal of property. In the Later Empire this was formulated in laws, as for example C.J.XI 48,23 (A.D.535): *Colonum alienum in suum ius suscipere*. Compare Salvian, *De gub. dei* V 38-39: *Pauperi ... dediticios se divitum faciunt et quasi in ius dicionemque transcedunt*.

42. Nov. XXXIII (to the praetorian prefect of Illyricum): *Propter avaritiam creditorum qui angustia temporum abutentes terrulas infelicium agrestium sibi adquirunt pro pauco frumento omnem illorum substantiam retinentes, legem posuimus, quam primo quidem in Thraciam et totas eius provincias, in praesenti autem in Illyricianas patrias direximus.*

43. C.J.XI 48,21. Earlier legislation clearly differentiates between these categories, as for instance Gaius IV 153: *Possidere autem videmur non solum si ipsi possideamus, sed etiam, si nostro nomine aliquis in possessione sit licet is nostro iuri subiectus non sit, qualis est colonus et inquilinus.*

societies, nor is it characteristic only of the Roman *colonus*.[44] It does not satisfactorily explain, however, all cases of dependent *coloni* who could not leave the land they cultivated without being punished. If the *coloni*, dependent as they were on the landlord by rent arrears and bound to his estate, were heterogeneous by origin, it would seem futile to search for a date and a single law from the Later Roman Empire that would suddenly tie them and other peasantry liable to taxation to the land. In fourth-century laws concerning taxes or punishment for attempted flight, various categories of *coloni* are differentiated. As the number of those who could no longer leave the land increased and they became the majority, the term *coloni* was sometimes used to refer to the entire agricultural population. *Liberi coloni* survived even in the Later Roman period; but they were bound to the *origo* as the agricultural population had been in the provinces from the beginning of the Roman rule, primarily through their fiscal obligations.

Coloni iuris alieni appear in the laws of the Later Roman Empire as a juristic status; different groups could come under this heading as do *adscripticii, inquilini* and the barbarians settled on the Roman soil.[45]

---

44. See Mitteis, *Volksrecht*; Finley, op. cit. in n. 36.

45. This paper is published in a slightly different form in Opus 5, 1986, 53ff.

ADSCRIPTICII:
CAPITA WITHOUT IUGERA

A*dscripticii* or *censibus adscripti*, the Greek ἐναπόγραφοι γεωργοί[1] are the terms most frequently used for dependent *coloni* in the Later Roman laws and in the papyrological documents from the fourth to seventh century. They were "added" to the tax declaration (*professio*) and description (*descriptio*) of the estate of the proprietor on whose land they worked. Probably the most numerous group among the *coloni; adscripticii* had no land of their own and, in arrears with their rent paying, were often *coloni iuris alieni*. Late in the fifth century, free unindebted *coloni* who had spent over 30 years on an estate were included by an act of the imperial administration in a group of *adscripticii*.

Laws from the fourth to sixth century frequently refer, directly or indirectly, to the position of *adscripticii* and their rights, primarily those related to disposition of property. The relationship with the *dominus fundi* was of marginal importance for the Roman state as far as the law was concerned, unless it impinged on the payment of taxes. Regulations focusing on this question reduced the rights of *adscripticii* and stressed their dependence on the landowner.

Dependence was not brought about by fiscal obligation. This is confirmed by a law of Arcadius and Honorius, directed to Neb-

---

1. The term *adscripticius* is documented for the first time in a law of A.D.224, C.J.VIII 51,1, which concerns the children of *ancillae* or *adscripticiae*, but is considered a later interpolation. The same explanation is applied to the *adscripticia condicio* in C.J.III 38,11, A.D.334. Eibach, *Kolonat* 142 and 204, thinks that *adscripticius* as a term denoting dependent *colonus* was not in use before the end of the fourth century; in the fifth and sixth centuries *adscripticius* would be "der bodengebundene, vom Grundherrn abhängige Pächter." The same author, op. cit., 137, distinguishes between those who were *censibus adscripti* and those who were *adscripticii*. It seems, however, that O. Seeck was right in ignoring differences in the basic meaning in all these terms, such as *adscripticii, censibus adscripti, censiti*, etc. The basic meaning of the word *adscripticius* is to denote someone who was *added* to somebody else's tax declaration, in contrast to the word *inscriptus*, denoting someone who existed in the tax-rolls under his own name and with his own land property. W. Buckland, *A Textbook of Roman Law*, 90f., and after him De Dominicis, *I coloni "adscripticii" nella legislatione di Giustiniano*, Studi in onore E. Betti III,1962,89ff. suggest that there were three ways of becoming *adscripticius:* by birth, by free acceptance of the position or by spending a long time as a tenant on another's land. Buckland adds *denuntiatio* as a fourth reason. Ἐναπόγραφος as corresponding to the Latin *adscripticius* is documented, except in the law, such as C.J.XI 48,19, on an inscription from Pisidia, CIL III 13640, A.D.527.

ridius proconsul of Asia about 396 A.D.[2], C.J.XI 50,2. That someone was registered on a landowner's tax declaration could not make his position better or worse; thus *coloni*, whether *censibus adscripti* or not, remained in a position closely resembling slavery: *Coloni censibus dutaxàt adscripti, sicuti ab his liberi sunt, quibus eos tributa subiectos non faciunt, ita his quibus annuis functionibus ac debito condicionis obnoxii sunt, paene est ut quadam servitute dediti videantur.*

The result was that the rights of the *coloni* were reduced, both with regard to their relations with the landowner to whom they were subjugated (*obnoxii*) and to the disposition of property (*peculium*). Since they could separate themselves neither from the landowner nor from the estate on which they worked, they could not sue those to whom the land belonged: *quo minus est ferendum, ut eos audeant lite pulsare, a quibus ipsos utpote a dominis una cum possessionibus distrahi posse dubium non est,* for how could the same rights apply to those whom the law did not even permit to dispose of property as they wished? *Cum enim saepissime decretum est, ne quid de peculio suo cuiquam colonorum ignorante domino praedii aut vendere aut alio modo alienare liceret, quemadmodum contra eius personam aequo poterit consistere iure, quem nec propria quidem leges sui iuris habere voluerint.* The *adscripticii* could not even bequeath their *peculia* to the church without consent of the *dominus fundi.* This right was restricted by C.Th.V 3,1 of A.D.434. Their *peculia* could only belong to the patrons or owners of the land to which they were tied: *bona quae ad eum pertinuerint, sacrosanctae ecclesiae vel monasterio cui fuerat destinatus, omnifariam socientur, exceptis his facultatibus, quas forte censibus adscripti vel iuri patronatus subiecti vel curiali condicioni obnoxii clerici monachive cuiuscumque sexus relinquunt. Nec enim iustum est bona seu peculia quae aut patrono legibus debentur aut domino possessionis cui quis eorum fuerat adscriptus ...ab ecclesias detineri.*[3]

The right to dispose of one's *peculium* is a characteristic of the *liberi coloni* and constitutes a significant difference between them and the *adscripticii* in Anastasius' law, C.J.XI 48,19 (A.D.491-518).

The Roman state regulated all prescriptions issued by law, always having in mind fiscal interests as the ultimate aim. Only the *adscripticius* could not be directly liable for tax as he did not have his own land and in the majority of cases could no longer dispose of his

---

2. As *proconsul Asiae* Nebridius is documented in C.Th.XI 30,56, of July 22, 396 A.D. and his title *comes* in C.J.XI 50,2 must be a mistake (see O. Seeck, *Regesten der Kaiser und Päpste* 10f., 27; Ensslin, RE *Suppl.* VII (1940), 550).

3. See the same in the *Acta conc.Chalc.*, ed. Schwarz, *Conc.Univ.Chalc.* vol .III, 1935,179: *neque potestatem habere monachos suscipere in suis monasteriis servos aut adscripticios sine voluntate dominorum.*

own *peculium*. The law of 366 A.D. requires the direct payment of tax by landowners, large and small.[4]   In the fourth century, those who worked another's land as free, unindebted tenants paid tax themselves, giving to the proprietor part of the yield from the land and keeping the rest as reward for their work. The *adscripticius* at that time did not have his own land and usually did not dispose of his own *peculium*. He therefore could not be entered on the tax-rolls under his own name and was not personally responsible for paying tax being in arrears with his rent and debts.[5] Taxes were always paid by the person to whom the land belonged, whether a *colonus* was entered in the *descriptio* under a declaration of taxes or was living on somebody's land as a fugitive, in the position of those who were *iuris alieni*. The law of Valentinianus and Valens from the 370s, C.J.XI 48,8, recalling all fugitives liable to taxation, clarifies the difference in liability between free *coloni* who obtained property and had the right to dispose of it and those who worked as *coloni iuris aleni*. In the case of a *colonus*—known to be *alienus* having been found on someone's estate—tax was paid to the state by the person who gave him shelter and who had the benefit of his work in the fields. This obviously meant *coloni* who were *adscripticii* and *alieni iuris*. If, however, the fugitives were represented as free *coloni*, *sui iuris ac liberi*, giving part of the fruits of the earth to the landowner and keeping the rest as reward for work, they were obliged to pay tax for the time that had elapsed.[6] In their new position, they obviously were not exploited as *coloni iuris alieni*, who had to be declared to the *census*. Since they were not *caput* on another's estate, they disposed of their property and were therefore personally liable for tax.

The *homologi*, too, could become *adscripticii* if they sank into the position of indebted *coloni*, just like the *inquilini*; in this position were also barbarians whom the Roman emperors had settled in Italy and in the provinces and above all the category of *coloni* known as *originarii*. Finally, free *coloni* also became *adscripticii* after 30 years' work on the same estate. The constitution prescribing this came down from Anastasius.

---

4. C.J.XI 48,4 (C.Th.1,14,A.D.372).

5. See Saumagne, *L'origo*, 508 f. See ch., Tax and Freedom.

6. C.J.XI 48,8:...*apud quos homines reperiuntur, alienos esse noverant fugitivos et profugis in lucrum suum usi sunt... ab illis tributa quae publicis perierunt functionibus exigantur.* and further: *Ceterum, si occultato eo profugi quod alieni esse videntur, quasi sui arbitri ac liberi apud aliquem se collocaverunt aut excolentes terras partem fructuum pro solo debitam dominis praestiterunt cetera proprio peculio reservantes, vel quibuscumque operis impensis mercedem placitam consecuti sunt, ab ipsis profugis quaecumque debentur exigantur.*

The *originates* or *originarii*[7] merit special attention, as in law of A.D.366, C.J.XI 48,4 they appear in a passage where one expects to find the term *adscripticius*. They were enrolled on the tax-rolls of a certain estate, whose owner was liable for tax: *Ii penes quos fundorum dominia sunt, pro his colonis originalibus quos in locis isdem censitos esse constabit, vel per se vel per actores proprios recepta compulsionis sollicitudine implenda munia functionis agnoscant.* *Originales* are contrasted here with those who paid taxes enrolled in the tax-rolls under their own name, *proprio nomine*. As the descendants of dependent *coloni*, they were entered as *capita* in the tax declaration of the person whose land they worked, and were therefore *adscripticii*. The terms *adscripticius* and *originarius*, however, were not synonymous. A.H.M. Jones considers that they signify two aspects of the same status: a man registered in a *census* list in the place where he belongs by birth. This harmonizes with his opinion that it was above all the descendants of *coloni* found on the land at the time of Diocletian's *census* who were bound to the land[8]—a logical conclusion, if we begin with the premise that the dependence of the *colonus* was created by administrative means. If however, we assume that the *coloni*, not as a class but as individuals, because of rent arrears and debt fell into dependence on those to whom the land belonged, it must be allowed that descendants of the *coloni* even after Diocletian could have been *originari*, if they inherited the status of their parents. Because many dependent *coloni* together with their families were entered in the *descriptio* of the estate, a law of A.D.388 requires that all fugitives should return to their original *penates* where they had been entered on the tax-rolls where they were born and brought up—*ubi censiri atque educati natique sunt.*[9]

The term *adscripticius* certainly has a broader meaning than *originarius*. A *colonus* who fell into dependency by himself and not through inheritance, could become *adscripticius*, as also could an *inquilinus* who was not *originarius*; barbarians settled on Roman territory were also obliged through their position as *tributarii* to be *adscripticii*. They did not have their own land and taxes for them was paid by those who received them on their estates.

The creation of the status of *adscripticius* was not the result of

---

7. Eibach, *Kolonat*, 205 ff., especially 214 ff. thinks that there is a distinction between *originarius* and *originalis*, only the first would mean the bound *colonus*.

8. Jones, *LRE* II 799: "The two terms, *originalis* and *adscripticius* merely express different aspects of the same situation, for the census registered man where he belonged by birth." See also the same, p.801.

9. C.J.XI 48,6: *Omnes omnino fugitivos adscripticios colonos vel inquilinos sine ullo sexus muneris condicionisque discrimine ad antiquos penates, ubi censiti atque educati natique sunt, provinciis praesidentes redire compellant.*

state or administrative pressure. There was evidently a strong tendency on the part of the landowner to enter *coloni* in the *descriptio* of
the estate at the time of the *census*, thus insuring labor for work in his
fields and state intervention in the case of runaway *coloni*. There were
of course *coloni* who were glad to place themselves under the
protection and patronage of powerful men and to transfer their fiscal
liability and responsibility to them. The state, however, preferred
free peasants and *coloni* entered under their own name (*proprio
nomine*) on the tax-rolls and who paid their own taxes. In A. D. 366
therefore a law prescribed that those who had land, regardless of its
size, should pay tax themselves.[10] Patronage was discouraged in the
fourth and early fifth centuries;[11] finally, at the time of Justinian, a
warning was issued that no one could be forced, either by agreement
or in writing, into *adscripticia condicio* and that this was invalid
without confirmation by the *census* inscription: *Cum scimus nostro
iure nullum praeiudicium generari cuidam circa condicionem neque ex
confessionibus neque ex scriptura, nisi etiam ex aliis argumentis aliquid
accesserit incrementum, sancimus solam condicionem vel aliam quam-
cumque scripturam ad hoc minime sufficere nec adscripticiam condicionem cuidam inferre, sed debere huiusmodi scripturae aliquid
advenire adiutorium quatenus vel ex publici census adscriptione vel ex
aliis legitimis modis talis scriptura adiuvetur.*[12]

The difference between *coloni* who remained free, who not
indebted to the landowner retained their right to dispose of their
peculium, and those who were "bound" to a certain *dominus fundi*,
lingered on into the fourth century and beyond as can be seen in laws
containing expressions such as *colonus vel adscripticius*.[13] Free *coloni*
could leave one landowner for another once they had carried out the
obligations undertaken under the lease contract; the *adscripticius*,
constrained by rental arrears, was entered in the landlord's tax
declaration and remained bound to a particular estate. In the law,
preserved only in its Greek version, Anastasius introduced a novelty:
liberi coloni, who once had spent 30 years on the same estate, were no

---

10. C.J.XI 48,4.

11. For *patrocinium*, see still basic work of F. de Zulueta, *De patrociniis vicorum, A
commentary on Codex Theodosianus XI 24 and Codex Iustinianus XI 54*, Oxford
Studies in Social and Legal History I,2,1909; L. Harmand, *Libanius, Discours sur les
patronages*, 1955. Cf. also G. Diosdi, *JJP* 14 (1962):57 ff; V. Dautzenberg, "Die
Gesetze des Codex Theodosianus und des Codex Iustinianus für Ägypten im Spiegel
der Papyri," Diss. Köln,1971,146ff.

12. C.J.XI 48,22.

13. See C.J.I 12, 6,9, 466 A.D.: *Sane si servus aut colonus vel adscripticius, familiaris
sive libertus et huiusmodi aliqua persona domestica vel condicioni subdita.*

longer able to leave it. The law emphasizes that they remained free and retained the right to dispose of their *peculium*, but could no longer leave the land; they become (*liberi*) *adscripticii* and paid taxes through the person to whom the land belonged. Thus, having to till the land and pay taxes, the law ultimately concludes, was useful both for the agricultural workers and landowners.[14]

This is the first appearance of a category of *coloni* bound not to the landowner, but to the land. Despite not having their own land, they were equated with those who did, the *liberi plebei*, being bound by fiscal obligation to the estate as if it belonged to them; on the other hand, because of the way in which they paid taxes, they were equated with dependent *coloni*. They were not entered on the tax-rolls under their own name, but under that of the landowner. Independence or freedom, as formulated by the laws, remained only in the disposition of property; they could no longer leave the land, although they were not in arrears with their rent.

After Anastasius, two groups of *adscripticii* must be taken into account: those who were dependent on the landowner, either because they sank to this position through rental arrears or because, as *originarii*, born on the estate, they inherited debt and dependence; the others were those who were bound to the land on which they had worked for 30 years by fiscal obligation. The laws differentiate between them: the former are called *alieni*, or *alieni iuris*, as the landlord is their *dominus*; the latter are *adscripticii* and do not belong to the landowner. In relation to them, he is the *dominus terrae* on which they work. If *alieni* or *adscripticii* escaped, it was the duty of the person on whose land they found shelter to bring them back: *Nemini autem liceat vel adscripticium vel colonum alienum scienti prudentique in suum ius suscipere. Sed et si bona fide eum susceperit, postea autem reppererit eum alienum esse constitutum, admonente domino vel ipsius adscripticii vel terrae et hoc faciente per se vel per procuratorem suum hunc restituere cum omni peculio et subole sua.*[15]

Basically, the dependence of someone who was a *colonus iuris alieni* was *debita condicio*; the other, *liber colonus*, was bound, as were peasants in general, only by fiscal obligation. The regulation that fugitive *adscripticii* were to be brought back together with their offspring, *cum subole sua*, refers equally to *coloni* who were *iuris alieni* and those who were *liberi coloni*. As a consequence of Justinian's decision, children of the free *adscripticii* must be *adscripticii*. Thus the status became hereditary. The decision, as formulated in the legal

---

14. C.J.XI 48,19.

15. C.J.XI 48,23,4 (Justinian, 531-534).

text from the third decade of the sixth century, C.J.XI 48,23,1, carries the stamp of true bureaucratic hypocrisy: first, children of free *coloni* who have spent 30 years on the same estate are also free and may not come into a worse position than that of their parents; second, they must remain on the land which their fathers once undertook to cultivate; they are bound to it and may not leave for another estate: *Cum autem Anastasiana lex homines qui per triginta annos colonaria detenti sunt condicione voluit liberos quidem permanere, non autem habere facultatem terra derelicta in alia loca migrare et ex hoc quae-rebatur, si etiam liberi eorum cuiuscumque sexus, licet non triginta annos fecerint in fundis vel vicis, deberent colonariae esse condicionis an tantum modo genitor eorum, qui per triginta annos huiusmodi condicioni illi-gatus est: sancimus liberos colonorum esse quidem in perpetuum secun-dum praefatam legem liberos et nulla deteriore condicione praegravari, non autem habere licentiam relicto suo rure in aliud migrare, sed semper terrae inhaerent, quam semel colendam patres eorum susceperunt.*[16]

There is no legal justification for this measure; a regulation that once bound dependent and indebted *coloni* is passed on to the children of independent, *liberi coloni*,who became *adscripticii* after thirty years of work on the same estate.

Taken by itself, Anastasius' law, by which even free *coloni* become bound to a certain estate on which they have worked for 30 years, is not inhuman. It protected a *colonus*, after such a long time spent on the same estate, as not even the *dominus fundi* could evict him when he was no longer in the full strength of his youth. However, his freedom to go where he would was irrevocably lost. In the age of Justinian the *adscripticius* could not be relieved of his status even when he carried out the duties of a curial or any other work; he remained bound to the same estate for life, *remaneat adscripticius et inhaeret terrae*, as stated in C.J.XI 48,23. It is likely that there was no strong desire to achieve freedom again. On the con-trary, literary and papyrological texts give examples of free peasants who placed themselves under the protection of powerful people, working on their estates as *adscripticii* or ἐναπόγραφοι.

For the children of *adscripticii*, there did remain one possibility of freeing themselves of this status. This is mentioned in Justinian's

---

16. There are many laws stipulating to which estate belong children born in wed-lock, in cases where one parent is *adscripticius/a* or *colonus/a*. A law of Constantine dating from 334 A.D., C.J. III 38,III states that children may not be divided in cases of division of property among heirs. The same emperor in a law C.J.XI 68,4 rules that children must remain in the place where their mother is domiciled. Cf. also later laws, C.Th. XII 19,1 (A.D.400), C.Th. X 20,17 (A.D.427), Nov. Valent. XXXI (451 A.D.) and others.

Novella 162,2: if born of a free mother, the son of an *adscripticius* is
a free *colonus*, but he cannot leave the land unless he acquires some of
his own, sufficient to earn a living. In this case, he becomes a free
peasant and is no longer *adscriptus* but *inscriptus censibus*, paying tax
by himself. In most cases, however, they had to stay *in vicos ipsos in
quibus orti sunt.*[17]

<h2 style="text-align:center">Ἐναπόγραφοι</h2>

The term *colonus adscripticius* appears in the Greek version of
some Later Empire constitutions as ἐναπόγραφος γεωργός, making
it possible to extend researches into this problem to papyrolog-ical
texts in which the term occurs frequently.[18] These documents are a
reflection of everyday life—in this the Egyptian ἐναπόγραφος
probably did not differ much from the *adscripticius* in the West—and
afford a possibility of studying things, unknown in the laws, which
had solved the problem of fiscal obligations in the first place.

Thereare a large number of documents from Egypt dealing with
the relations between those called ἐναπόγραφοι and those who were
landowners, δεσπόται. Regulations contained in papyrological texts
on the duties of the ἐναπόγραφος or his relationship to the
δεσπότης do not contradict what we can glean from the legal texts in
the Codes. Many contracts envisage penalties for an ἐναπόγραφος
who does not fulfill his obligations or who leaves the estate on which
he has to work. Cases sometimes refer to γεουχικὸς λόγος which

---

17. Whether the same rule was applied also on *coloni* themselves, is difficult to prove.
In this sense could be interpreted the passage in Nov.Iust. 128,14: *Nullus autem
penitus molestetur pro tributis terrarum quas non possidet, sed etiam si contingat
agricultores alicui competentes aut inscriptos propriam habere possessionem, illos pro ea
publica exigi tributa, domino eorum nullam pro ea molestiam sustinente, nisi forte
propria voluntate tali functioni se fecit obnoxium.*

18. Except in the laws of Anastasius and Justinian, C.J.XI 48,19 and 23, *adscripticius*
is translated as ἐναπόγραφος; also in bilingual inscription from Pisidia, CIL III
13640, dating from 527 A.D. Without wishing to give a complete list here are some
of the most typical examples: P.Miln. 64 = SB VI 9503; cf. S. Daris, Aegyptus 37,
1957,92 ff (A.D.440/445); P.Oxy. 2724 (A.D. 469); P.Oxy.1899 (A.D. 476); P.Oxy.
1983 (A.D.535); P.Oxy.1985 (A.D.543); P.Brit.Mus. 776 (A.D.568); P.Brit. Mus. 774
(A.D.582); P.Oxy.1988 (A.D.787); P.Oxy. 1990 (A.D.591); P.Oxy.135 (A.D.579);
P.Oxy.1979 (A.D.613) and others. Johnson and West, *Byzantine Egypt*, 29ff. consider
that these were contracts between *enapographos* and the proprietor and divide these
documents under the following headings: receipts for parts for agricultural
machinery; contracts on lending money to the *colonus* by the pro-prietor; deeds of
surety guarantee that the *enapographos* would remain on the estate and pay liturgies.
They suppose that ἐναπόγραφος in those documents does not correspond to the
Latin *adscripticius* referred to in the laws of Justinian.

could be either usual practice or general Roman law. However, no text contains the slightest indication that anyone was forced to become an ἐναπόγραφος: this was a position taken up voluntarily, often at his own request and with undertaking or carrying out all the obligations it entailed. This is the major contribution made by papyrological sources to the study of this problem.

Papyrological documents are most frequently in the form of some kind of receipt from ἐναπόγραφος for the purchase of parts for irrigation machinery or requests to be taken onto an estate, or to be taken back after running away. In both cases, the ἐναπόγραφοι humbly stress their willingness to carry out their obligations and all that would be asked of them, and to pay their φόρος regularly. Although there are documents which contain no guarantee for fulfillment of obligation, there is a large group called "Deeds of surety" by modern editors, in which a third party or one group of ἐναπόγραφοι for another guarantees that the first party will remain on the estate and carry out all that is required of them.

Most numerous in the former group of documents are those referring to the purchase of wheels and other parts for irrigation machinery. P.Oxy.1982 (497 A.D.) is a fairly typical example. The text is from Aurelius Josephus, son of Abraam, ἐναπόγραφος γεωργός on the estate ἐποικία of Papsaos to a landowner Flavius Strategius from the town of Oxyrhynchus. The ἐναπόγραφος confirms that he has received an axle for an irrigation machine and undertakes to pump water and irrigate in a proper manner, to pay φόρος and to be obedient in all things as regulated by γεουχικὸς λόγος: ὁμολογῶ τὰς ἀντλήσεις καὶ ὑδροπαροχείας ἀμέμπτως ποιεῖσθαι καί τοὺς φόρους εὐγνωμ[ο]νεῖ καὶ ὑπακούειν εἰς ἅπαντα τὰ ἀνήκοντα τῳ γεουχικῷ λόγῳ.[19]

From this and similar documents it is clear that these are people working another's land. They seem not to have *instrumentum* but rather to be purchasing irrigation machinery on behalf of the person to whom the land belongs. That no property is mentioned by way of guarantee means that they did not have any and were therefore dependent.

Requests from ἐναπόγραφοι gives a better picture of their position. Evidence of the sorry state in which one fugitive found himself after three years spent abroad (ἐπὶ ξένῃ) is afforded by a passage from P.Oxy.2479 (sixth century). It contains interesting

---

19. For the meaning of the word ἐποικία see Lewuillon-Blume, XV Pap.Kongr.- 1979, 177ff. The same meaning has the word κτῆμα in some documents, cf. G. Bastianini, *Papyrologica florentina* 7, 1980, commentary ad P.Oxy.996.

information on the fiscal and other obligations of the ἐναπόγραφος:
Pieous from the ἐποικίον of Kineas who calls himself a slave
ὑμετέρου δοῦλος, admits that he left the land three years before
because, as he states in his request to be taken on again, his cattle had
died.[20] Then, when he returned and had resown the land he had
previously tilled in order to raise his children, a προνοητής arrived
and confiscated all his property because he had not paid his dues, καὶ
τοῦτο δὲ διδάσκω ὡς ὅτι ἐλθὼν ἐν τῷ κτήματι ὁ προνοητής
διήρπαξεν πάντα τὰ εὐτελῆ μοῦ πράγματα χάριν τῆς
τοιαύτης αἰτίας. The passage ends with a plea by the ἐναπόγραφος
to the landlord to help him, as due to εὐθενία neither he or his
children have a crust of bread to eat: τὸ ξηρὸν ψῶμιν οὐκ ἔχω
φαγεῖν μετὰ τῶν ἐμῶν τέκνων προκειμένης τ[αύ]της [ἐνε]κα
τῆς εὐθενίας.

The key words in the interpretation of this text are συντελεῖν,
προνοητής and εὐθενία. J.Triantaphylopoulos draws attention to
them in a short article dated 1967.[21] The verb συντελεῖν which the
editor of this document, John Rea, understands as "to pay rent,"
Triantaphylopoulos prefers to link to the payment of tax. The first
interpretation, in his opinion, would not be impossible, but it is less
likely; the verb is closely linked to the noun συντελεία and apart
from one exception, always means the payment of tax.[22] If we start
then from the usual sense of συντελεία and συντελεῖν, then the
term προνοητής would also belong to the group of concepts referring to tax payment: he would not be the private agent of the
landowner who collects rent and tax, but an official tax collector.
This is confirmed by another verb in the passage, ἀπαιτηθῆναι
which at that time would have meant primarily "to demand tax," that

---

20. J.G. Keenan returns to this text in ZPE (1980):246ff., improving the reading in
several points. Two corrections have a bearing on the question which is of interest
here: line 20, where οὐ at the beginning of the line changes to ἄν so that instead of
δύνατος γὰρ ἔχω δέσποτα συντελέσαι ὑπὲρ οὐ οὐ σπείρω "for I cannot,
lord, pay on what I do not sow," we get ἀδύνατος γὰρ ἔχω, δέσποτα, συντελέσαι ὑπὲρ οὗ ἄν σπείρω "For I am unable, master, to pay contributions for
what I sow." The meaning would be that he has sown, but is unable to pay the
demands of the tax exactor and so requests exemption from all levies.

21. J..Triantaphylopoulos, εὐθηνία, P.Oxy. 2479, REG 80,1967, 355ff.

22. Ibid., 356: "Συντελεῖν peut signifier "payer le fermage ..seulement si nous con-
cedons à συντελεία (non au verbe συντελεῖν) la signification rarissime de pensio
= fermage, qu'on rencontre ἅπαξ dans les Glossae Latino-Graecae (Corpus Closs.
Lat.II 145,20). On peut donc douter à juste raison, que συντελέσαι puisse signifier
dans le papyrus 'payer le fermage'."

it was paid in kind.[23] Finally, εὐθενία could also be interpreted in the same way. The first editor of the text, considering that this word basically means *abundance* or *supplying with grain* and unable to incorporate it into a text which speaks of hunger, proposes that it should be supplanted by word ἀσθενεία and translates line 26ff. as follows: "I have not a morsel to eat, nor my children, because of this helplessness (?) that I have mentioned." Triantaphylopoulos returns again to the basic meaning of the word εὐθηνία and finding it close to the Latin *annona*, thus links it to tax, as well as words συντελεῖν and προνοητής. This would then mean that the ἐναπόγραφος in this document had to pay tax, not rent and so turns to the landowner to protect him from the severity of the state tax collector.

Triantaphylopoulos is certainly right in his interpretation when he returns to the original text with εὐθηνία and its basic meaning, equivalent to the Latin *annona*.[24] It seems, however, that the word should not be understood only as tax owed to the state. When interpreting this text, it must be borne in mind that it deals with someone who was ἐναπόγραφος and therefore not entered under his own name on the tax-rolls, but in the *professio* of the land-owner. In such cases, tax was not gathered by state tax collectors but by the agents of the landlord, as formulated by a law of 366 A.D.[25] Προνοητής in the passage from P.Oxy.2479 could have been one of these agents which would explain why the complaint concerning εὐθενία was directed to the landowner, προνοητής probably de-manded not only tax but rent from the returned ἐναπόγραφος; this is what in other papyrological documents from Egypt is designated by plural, φόροι or ἐκφορία.[26] That the προνοητής collected both, tax and rent, may be seen from the text dated A.D.583, P.Oxy. 583: προνοητής undertakes on the one hand to collect tax on the estate—obviously paid in kind—and load it into ships and on the other hand to deposit rent in the form of cash in the landlord's bank.[27]

---

23. Triantaphylopoulos, 359.

24. See Preisigke, *Wörterbuch*, s.v. Εὐθηνια and Bd. III Abschnitt 11.

25. C.J.XI 48,4: *Ii penes quos fundoram dominia sunt pro his colonis originalibus quos in locis isdem censitos esse constabit, vel per se vel per actores proprios recepta compul-sionis sollicitudine implenda munia functionis agnoscant.*

26. See e.g. P.Oxy.2478. In the text PSI 62 the, term δημοσία also occurs.

27. Line 19ff. εἰς τὸ πάντα εἰσπράξαι καὶ καταβαλεῖν ἐπὶ τὴν ὑμῶν ὑπερφυειαν ἤτοι ἐπὶ τοὺς αὐτῇ προσήκοντας τοῦτ ἐστιν τὸν μὲν σῖτον ἐ[π]ὶ τ[ὸ] δεμόσιον ναύτεν τοῦ ἐνδόξου αὐτῆς οἴκου. Despite his conclusion that the *pronoetes* was a tax collector, Triantaphylopoulos translates the word once as "intendant de son patron," p.355, and on another occasion as "percepteur d'impôt,"

This information on the προνοητής duty—he was indisputably in the private service of the estate owner—helps us to understand both, εὐθενία and συντελεῖν on P.Oxy.2479. This was an issue only of tax payment; by all appearances it covered everything the ἐναπόγραφος was obliged to pay. The rent remained with the land-owner while the tax was sent to the state treasure.

Ἐναπόγραφοι did not have their own land, but they did own cattle—this was expected of them just as it was expected of the *coloni* in the earlier centuries—to have *instrumentum*.[28] Initially, the Pieous mentioned in P.Oxy 2479 had cattle, but when they died, he was no longer able to till the land and therefore left it. It is possible that he had other property that could be considered *peculium* and which doubtless served to guarantee that he would carry out the obligations contained in the lease contract. When after three years he returned to the estate he had abandoned, the προνοητής, evidently because of rental arrears and overdue tax, took all that he had.

The cattle with which the ἐναπόγραφος worked in the fields was his principle property, as may seen from other papyrological documents. Among them one from the fourth century, P.Oxy.130, is interesting for a number of reasons. This is an ἐναπόγραφος who borrowed a large sum of money in order to buy cattle, his own having died. As he did not return the money in time, he fell into the difficult position of an indebted *colonus*.[29] He tried to induce mercy in the landowner from whom he had borrowed the money: "Let thy mercy spread also over me," it reads, "for unless your pity extends to me, my lord, I cannot stay on my holding and serve the interest of the state."[30]

The text in fact refers to an ἐναπόγραφος whose father and ancestors had worked on the same estate. He calls himself the owner's slave and says that his forebears served the same master and paid tax l. 77ff:

---

p.356. In fact this term denoted the people whom the law from 366, C.J. XI 48,4 calls *actores*. They collected tax from *coloni* who were *originales*.

28. *Instrumentum* of the *coloni* in the *Digesta*: XXXIII 7,20; XXXIII 7,2.

29. He is not explicitly designed as an ἐναπόγραφος in the text, but it is clear from the context that he was.

30. See line 16ff.: οὐ δύναμαι σταθῆναι ἐν τῷ ἐμῷ κτήματι καὶ χρησιμεῦσαι τοῖς γεουχικος πράγμασιν. In documents of this kind, the ἐναπόγραφος often denotes the land he works as his own. This simply emphasizes that this was the land given to him to work on it. In this case the ἐναπόγραφος owed the landowner 15 *solidi*. For Appion's estate, see J. Gascou, "Les grands domaines, la cité et l'etat en Egypte byzantine," *Travaux et mémoires*, Collège de France, Centre de recherche d' histoire et civilisation de Byzance 9, (1985),1ff. and *Appendix* I, p.61ff.

ὅθενκἀγὼ ὁ ἐλεεινὸς δοῦλος τοῦ ἐμοῦ ἀγαθοῦ δεσπότου
μοῦ διὰ ταύτης τῇ [ς] παρούσης δεησεήσεως ἐλεηθῆναί
μοι βούλομαι γνῶναι τὴν ὑμετέραν δεσποτίαν ὡς ἐκ
πατέρων καὶ ἐκ προγόνων δουλεύειν τῷ ἐμῷ δεσπότῃ
πλερῶσαι ἐτησίως τὰ δημόσια.

If we sum up the content of P.Oxy.130, we may come to the following conclusion: Anoup, who begs for mercy from the well-known great estate owner Apion, paid tax, τὰ δημόσια, to the landlord and not to the state directly, showing that this was an ἐναπόγραφος γεωργός or *adscripticius colonus*. Since he was indebted, he no longer disposes of his own property (in this case cattle) and therefore was not a free *colonus* but one of the *iuris alieni*. That is why he calls himself ὁ δοῦλος τοῦ ἐμοῦ δεσπότου. He is also *originarius*, as his father and ancestors had worked too on the same estate.

It seems that taxation was not the main factor that brought Anoup close to slavery, although he paid it through an intermediary; it was the result of his indebtedness. The mere fact of working on another's land, paying both rent and tax, could not lead to a reduction of freedom. A fourth century papyrological text, P.Ross.Georg.III,8 proves this. Addressing someone whom they call both δεσπότης and κύριος, peasants from the village of Eumeria point out: "We wish thee to know, our lord Nebo that we have given over our bodies neither to thy father nor to thy goodness; every year we pay ἐντάγιον,[31] we are subjugated to no one.

There were many ways of guaranteeing that an ἐναπόγραφος would carry out his obligations. First, those who were free *coloni* disposed of their own *peculium* and therefore used it as a guarantee. In this manner eight ἐναπόγραφοι in P.Oxy.1896 (A.D.577) from the ἐποικίον of Leo on Apion's estate, declare that from the harvest in the month of Mesoru on the tenth of indiction they will pay 3.000 pithos of wine against current rent and arrears. This they guarantee by pledging their property.[32] Third-party guarantees that the ἐναπόγραφος would fulfill his obligations were a commonplace occurrence. These must have been indebted and dependent ἐναπόγραφος. An

---

31. Ἐντάγιον could be a private payment ("privater Zahlungsauftrag"), or a tax payment, ("Steuererhebungsauftrag") Preisigke, *Worterbuch*,s.v.

32. This is a rare evidence of a rent owing, σὺν τῇ λοιπάδι τοῦ ἐκλόγου τῆς παρούσης ἰνδύ. in line 19. Deeds of surety pledging property, κυνδίνω τῶν ἡμῖν ὑπάρχ(οντων) as in the *paramoné* contracts, are known from many other documents, as for instance P.Oxy. 3204 (A.D. 588) P.Oxy. 2478 (A.D.595 or 596), P.Heid. 248 (VI/VII century) etc.

example of a simple contract of this kind is the instance of P.Wisc.I 12 of A.D.345: Aurelius Paris, son of Harpocratis from the village of St. Amata, guarantees to Aurelius Achilles, who was *prytanos, gymnasiarchos* and councillor at Oxyrhynchos, that Aurelius Aion, son of Aion, a wine-grower from the same village, will remain on the estate and will cultivate it; at the end of the document he swears to God that he will bear the consequences if the former does not fulfill all that is required of him.[33]

Later contracts of this kind were more involved and envisaged that the surety in the case of ἐναπόγραφος failing to fulfill his obligations or leaving the land, should either pay a sum of money to the landowner or himself perform all what was expected of the ἐναπόγραφος. In any case, the guarantor undertook to return the fugitive and to hand him over to the custody or prison of the landlord. P.Oxy. 135 of 579 A.D. is typical in this group of deeds sureties. Line 10ff. says:

> I agree of my own free will, under oath by Heaven and the Emperor to be surety and pledge to your magnificence, through your representatives, for Aurelius Abraham, son of Herminus and Herais, who comes from the estate Great Tarouthinus belonging to your magnificence in the Oxyrhynchite nome, and is entered as your ἐναπόγραφος. I engage that he shall continually abide and stay on his holding along with his kin[34] and wife and herds and all his possessions, and be responsible for all that regards his person or the fortunes of him who has been entered as a cultivator; and that he shall in no wise leave his holding or remove to another place, and if he is required of me by your magnificence through your representatives at any date

---

33. Line 11ff., ὑποστῆναι τὰ πρὸς αὐ[τὸ]ν [ζ]ητούμενα; cf. similar on BGU III 936, P.Wurzb.16,SB 9152 and alia. In some documents of this kind, the guarantor undertakes, should he fail to deliver the *enapographos*, to be himself ὑπεύθυνος, e.g. PSI I 61 and 62, P.Mert.98, P.Heid. 306 and others, from various epochs from the fourth to the seventh century, and in some of them that he will accept the status of ἐναπόγραφος, as for instance P.Oxy. 135, line 17ff.: μετὰ τῶν αὐτοῦ φιλτάτων καὶ γαμετῆς καὶ κτηνῶν καὶ πάσης τῆς αὐτοῦ ἀποσκευῆς ἀποκρινόμενον εἰς ἅπαντα τὰ ὁρῶντα τὸ αὐτοῦ πρό[σ]ωπον ἤτοι τὴν τοῦ ἐναπογράφου τύχην.

34. Μετὰ τῶν αὐτοῦ φιλτάτων καὶ γαμετῆς in line 17 the editor translates as "along with his friends and wife." In fact this is the same as what legal texts call *agnatio*, when they prescribe the return of dependent *coloni* to the estate where they were registered in the tax-rolls, e.g. C.J.XL 52,1, *cum omni peculio suo et agnatione*. Cf. also C.J.III 38,11 and C.Th. II 25,1. The above-mentioned phrase in some papyri is interpreted in this sense, as for example P.Heid.248: "mit seinen Angehörigen und seiner Frau," or P.Mert. II 98: "With their families and property."

or for any reason whatsoever, I will bring him forward and produce him in a public place without any attempt at flight or excuse, in the keeping of your same honoured house just as he is now when I become his surety. If I do not do this I agree to forfeit for his non-appearance and my failure to produce him 8 gold solidi, actual payment is to be enforced."

There are documents in which the guarantor undertakes to pay φόρος in case the ἐναπόγραφος for whom he has pledged leaves the land: Zacharias, son of Anastasius, οἰκονόμος of the church of the Ascension in Oxyrhynchos on P.Oxy.2478 (595 or 596 A.D.) guarantees that Aurelius Pambechios from the ἐποικίον of Athlites on the estate of Flavius Apion, will remain on the land as an ἐναπόγραφος and that he will as πώμαριος cultivate an orchard and pay φόρος every year; should he fail to do this and leave the land and Zacharias as guarantor fail to return him, the latter shall compensate for ἐκφορία for what he pledges his entire property l.26ff.: εἰ μὴ τοῦτο ποιήσω ὁμολογῶ οἴκοθεν [ὑπ]ὲρ αὐτοῦ πληρῶσαι τὰ ἐκφόρια τοῦ αὐτοῦ γεουχικοῦ πωμαρίου κινδύνῳ ἐμῷ καὶ τῆς πάσης μοῦ ὑποστάσεως.

Another widespread practice was mutual surety among ἐναπόγραφοι, one pledging for another or a group for another group.[35] Thus, for example, Aurelius Pasoeris and Aurelius Joannes pledge for each other with the owner of the estate Flavia Kyria from Oxyrhynchos that they will pump water and irrigate the land; in the case of one failing to do so, the other will perform it in his stead, P.Oxy. 2724: προσομολο[γοῦμεν] ἐξ ἀλλελεν[γύη]ς τὰς ἀντλήσεις καὶ ὑδροπαρ[ο]χί[ας π]οιειθαι ἀ[μ]εμπτως. On another document from 609 A.D., PSI 61, Jeremiah, son of Josephus from the ἐποικίον of Panguleeia, an ἐναπόγραφος himself makes surety for another, Aurelius Pamoun of the same *epoikion,* that the latter will remain on the estate of Flavius Apion and will never under any pretext abandon it; should he fail to do so, Jeremiah will return and hand him over to the guard of the honorable house. If he does not succeed in this, he himself will take up a position of a subordinate laborer (ὑπεύθυνος) and answer for all what was required of the other: εἰ δὲ μὴ τοῦτο ποιήσω [ὁμολ]ογῶ ὑ[π]εύθυνος πᾶσιν

35. Cf. PSI I 59,61,62; P.Lond.III 778,p.279; SB XII 10944; P.Oxy.1979. P.Oxy.996 also deals with this, to which two papers published simultaneously are devoted: G. Bastianini, "Miscellanea Papyrologica," *Papyrologica florentina* 7 (1980):25ff. and I.F. Fikhman, ibid. 67ff. The former gives a list of deeds of surety, op. cit. 26. A list of such documents may also be found in Wilcken, *Archiv für Papyrusforschungen* 1, 1901, and in the commentary of P.Heid.IV p.91ff.

τοῖς πρὸ [ς αὐτὸν] ἐπιζητουμέ(νοις) ἀποκρίνασαι.

The surety ἐναπόγραφος and the person for whom he gave surety were often not in the same position. There are several instances that demonstrate this, among them P.Oxy.996, in which three ἐναπόγραφοι one of whom is πρεσύβτερος and another φροντιστής, guarantee for another two, or P.Brit.Mus. III 778, in which the ἐναπόγραφος Georgios, a διάκονος, guarantees for another. In both cases, however, the end has not been preserved, so that it is not known whether they pledged their property or to work in the other's stead. Here there may have been two categories of ἐναπόγραφοι: those who were dependent and indebted correspond to what Later Roman legislation called *coloni iuris alieni* and *adscripticii*; the others, who disposed of their *peculia* were the same as *coloni* or *adscripticii liberi* in the laws of Anastasius and Justinian.

There are other circumstances indicating that ἐναπόγραφοι for whom others guaranteed were in fact dependent *coloni*, i.e. *iuris alieni*. One such circumstance is that in the case of flight from the land, it was the guarantor who was to return the fugitive, first to a public place and then ἐν φυλακῇ . This latter regulation merits special attention. Interpretation is uncertain and editors translate it in various ways, as for instance "in the keeping of your same honoured house,"[36] "in the guard room of your said honourable house"[37] or simply "in the prison."[38] This last, which imposes itself as the first and most natural interpretation and which Preisigke accepts for this kind of texts,[39] is hard to reconcile with legal regulations concerning prisons. First, many documents deal with the φυλακή of the landlord, as for example P.Oxy 130, ἐν τῇ φυλακῇ τοῦ ἐνδόξου οἴκου or ἐν φυλακῇ τοῦ αὐτοῦ Κέλους in P.Mert.II 98. Second, in some texts φυλακῇ τῆς αὐτῆς πόλεως appears, as for example in P.Oxy 3204.[40]

As early as 320 A.D. the law made prisons official institutions, created for criminals; a law of 388 A.D. warned those holding people in private custody that they would be charged with violating state authority; the Emperor Zeno in 486 A.D. issued orders that no one in Alexandria and the Egyptian dioceses or any other province, could have a private prison, either in his house or on his land; finally,

---

36. P.Oxy.135.

37. A.S. Hunt and C.C. Edgar, *Selected papyri* I 26,p.79.

38. E.R. Hardy, *The large Estates* 69, n.2.

39. Cf. Preisigke, *Wörterbuch* s.v.

40. See for others examples, Fikhman, Papyr.flor. 7,74 ad line 16 and 76, ad lines 17-18.

Justinian, repeating this prohibition, ordained that anyone who did not submit to it would himself spend in a public prison as many days as he had held another person in his private one.[41] There can be no doubt that this was a widespread phenomenon. However, it can hardly be expected that private imprisonment is being threatened in the documents such as deeds of surety dealt with here. The interpretation of φυλακή as prison in such cases cannot be reconciled with another circumstance: the ἐναπόγραφοι here had to work on the land of the proprietor; for thus, keeping them in prison would be pointless. This is emphasized by the law of Emperors Honorius and Theodosius, prohibiting *coloni* to leave the land under any pretext or for any period of time.[42] Keeping them in prison must also have been forbidden, as they had to work in the fields.

If φυλακή did not literally mean prison, it still meant a restriction on the freedom of ἐναπόγραφοι who attempted to leave the land. These being in the same position as *coloni iuris alieni* in Roman legal texts, the word φυλακή could have originated with them. Constantine in 332 A.D., C.Th.V 17, 1 ordered that *coloni* who intended to escape must be put in irons *(ferro ligari)* and carry out their tasks of free people in conditions envisaged for slaves. Similar decrees exist in later laws.[43] Ἐναπόγραφοι who attempted to evade their obligations could be treated in the same way: once returned, they had to carry out their duties on the estate as *vincti*.

This explanation cannot be applied to the city jail mentioned in some documents. This, if indeed it really was a prison, might have been a temporary measure, used until the ἐναπόγραφος was returned to the landowner. Official procedure, it could be said, was envisaged for other cases, too, since it is always mentioned that the fugitive shall be first taken to a public place and then handed over to the guard or to prison.[44]

---

41. C.Th.XI 7,3 (A.D.320), C.Th.VIII ll,l (A.D.388),C.J.IX 5,1 (A.D.486) and C.J.IX 5,2 (A.D. 529).

42. C.J.XI 48,15: *Imp. Honorius et Theodosius AA.Probo. Colonos numquam fiscalium nomine debitorum ullius exactoris pulset intentio. Quos ita glebis inhaerere praecipimus, ut ne puncto quidem temporis debeant amoveri.*

43. Cf. C.J.XI 53,1 (A.D.371): *revocati vinculis poenisque subdantur.*

44. Hardy, *Large Estates*, 69, n.2 considers that this refers to two procedures: first, bringing to a public place and then delivery to custody; Fikhman, op.cit. in note 35, p.75, ad line 17, suggests a more complex procedure: the guarantor first brings the *enapographos* to a public place; he then goes to prison from which the guarantor redeems him, paying bail. In the latter Fikhman sees the essence of the surety. It is true that he allows of another possibility: that for the official scribe "a public place" was a prison of a large estate. It would seem, however, that δημόσιος τόπος and φυλακή τῆς πόλεως could have been one and the same, as could also be inferred

It is clear that the guarantor to a certain extent disposed of the person of the ἐναπόγραφος for whom he pledged: he gave him into the service of another and guaranteed that he would fulfill all that was required of him. This shows that the ἐναπόγραφος was dependent on the guarantor. On the other hand, the guarantor must have been dependent on the landowner to whom he guaranteed that another one would work on his land. The guarantor also stipulated that, if the ἐναπόγραφος left the land and he failed to return him, he would himself compensate for his work as ὑπεύθυνος the position occupied by the fugitive.

In some deeds of surety, the guarantor paid a certain sum in the case of failing to return the ἐναπόγραφος to the landowner. This seems to be of importance in explaining the substance of the deeds of surety. The sums are different on two of these documents which, chronologically speaking, are relatively close to each other: P.Oxy. 135 refers to 8 gold *solidi* and P.Oxy. 3204— to two Alexandrian gold ounces; the first dates from 579 and the second from 588 A.D. Since the amounts vary, it is not very likely that there was any standard fine. It may rather have been a debt by the guarantor to the landlord. This is what seems to be at issue in deeds of surety which pledge entire properties, such as the *paramoné* contracts. It might therefore be concluded that deeds of surety from various periods, from the fourth to the sixth centuries, reflect many types of dependency: guarantees by landlords, ἐναπόγραφοι by guarantors. This could be the procedure known in Roman law as *delegatio:* the guarantor in P.Oxy.135, for example, may have owned the large land possessor Apion 8 *solidi;* instead of returning them, he gives him an ἐναπόγραφος to work off his debt, because he was indebted to him. In other words, A is indebted to B, but transfers his obligation to a third, C, who then works off his debt to A, but on land belonging to B. If this is so, then the basic issue was of debts and working them off.[45]

---

from a phrase in SB 9152 (A.D.492) or CPR V 17,13 (late fifth century): δημόσιος τόπος ταύτης τῆς πόλεως. That on the other side δημόσιος τόπος and φυλακή on the estate could be two different things, is evident from a phrase in P.Oxy.2238, lines 16-18: ἐν δημοσίᾳ ἐπὶ ταύτης τῆς πόλεως ἐκτὸς ἁγίων περιβόλων καὶ θείων χαρακτήρων καὶ πάντος τόπον προσφυγῆς ἄνθα αὐτὸν καὶ παρειλήφαμεν ἐν τῇ φυλακῇ.

45. In P.Oxy.2420, from 620 A.D. one gold libra appears as a sum to be paid by the guarantor in the case of failing to return the *enapographos* but the text is extensively damaged and supplemented by analogy to some preserved texts. None of these can refer to a fine prescribed by law; in this case the amount could be expected to remain the same, as in fourth-century laws on the sheltering of another's *colonus,* C.Th. V 17,2, A.D.386 (6 ounces for keeping a private *colonus,*1 libra for *patrimonialis*) or in C.J.XI 52,2 (two libras as damages to the owner from whose estate the *colonus* fled).

The papyrological documents quoted here permit us to conclude that there were two categories of ἐναπόγραφοι: those who could dispose of property, if they had it, corresponding to those who appear in legal texts as *liberi adscripticii*;[46] the others were dependent and correspond to the *coloni iuris alieni* mentioned in laws of the Later Roman Empire. Common to both was the indirect payment of tax through the person to whom the land belonged. This was done through an agent who could be the προνοητής, as attested in some papyrological documents. The position of ἐναπόγραφος is clearly defined in papyrological texts, primarily in deeds of surety: he may not leave the land he has undertaken to cultivate; he does not dispose of the property with which he came to the estate; he is ὑπεύθυνος who must carry out what the landlord requires of him; his position is designated as ἐναπογραφὴ τύχη which undoubtedly corresponds to the Latin *condicio adscripticia;* ultimately, if he leaves the land, he is returned by force and may literally be bound or imprisoned.[47]

The essence of the status of ἐναπόγραφος or *adscripticius* comes down to two things: his relation to the landowner and to the payment of taxes. The former was never regulated by law, but rather by agreement or private contract. Anyone working on another's land property undertook a series of obligations for the fulfillment of which he pledged either his entire property, his labor or his person, as was frequently the case with the "descendants of the Persians" in the *paramoné* documents. Since these are private contracts, this is always an agreement, or petitions from ἐναπόγραφοι to be taken on the estate to work as humble ὑπεύθινοι δοῦλοι and similar subordinate people and not a forcible binding of the person either to the landowner or to the land. Penalities are envisaged in the case of nonfulfillment of obligation on the part of an ἐναπόγραφος or *adscripticius.*

---

46. I.G. Fikhman, Proceed. XVI Pap.Congr.1980,471, considers that deeds of surety should certainly not be interpreted as expressions of mistrust on the part of the landlord towards the peasants or as a sign that *coloni* were deprived of the legal opportunity to undertake obligations towards landowners; he also disputes M. Palasse's interpretation of the surety "a contract on the *adscripticii* relationship" (*Orient et Occident,* 67) and considers that this was a guarantor who has redeemed an *enopographos* from jail by paying bail. This would have done in his capacity as a member of the peasants association, κοινὰ τῶν γεωργῶν. For deeds of surety, see also O. Montevecchi, *La papirologia* (1973):192ff. and a more recent brief review in P.Heid. IV 91ff.

47. These texts do not explicitly state that it was flight of the *enapographos* from the land on which he was obliged to stay and to perform what was asked from him, but it is clear from the context that this was in the question, as for instance P.Oxy.135, line 28: ὁμολογῶ καταβαλεῖν ὑπὲρ τῆς αὐτοῦ ἀπολείψεως.

Payment of taxes is regulated by the law from the time when the problem of how to tax land worked by those to whom it did not belong arose. Fiscal liability did not bring about the dependence of the *coloni* but did contribute to its becoming widespread. Rigorous measures taken against tax debtors had the effect that those with little land and large taxes and other debts sought refuge on large estates as *adscripticii*. According to the testimony of Salvianus, *De gub. dei* V 8,43 rapacious demands by tax exactors drove many small freeholders in Gaul to seek safety and shelter as *coloni* on wealthy estates. They lost their land possessions, but they remained to work on it as *coloni*. There are also examples from Egypt of some remaining in the status of ἐναπόγραφος to work on land which once belonged to them.[48]

Harsh reality created the conviction even among *coloni* of this type that their position was close to slavery, and they refer to themselves in petitions to the landlord as slaves (δοῦλοι) and to their service on another's land as slavery (δουλεία); to them the landowner is master (δεπότης, κύριος) to whom they undertake not to leave the land, to obey him in all things and to pay φόρος. It seems, however, that this applied mainly to dependent *adscripticii*, who because of their debts to the landlord had lost their property and the right to dispose of it. Free *adscripticii* / ἐναπόγραφοι were in a better position. Personal dependency on the landowner was not automatically transferred to them, even when, after thirty years' work on the same estate, they could no longer leave it. The difference between them and those who were dependent was to remain until the sixth century; it is visible in legal formulations such as *adscripticius vel colonus alienus*, either *adscripticius* or an indebted, dependent *colonus*, C.J.XI 48,4.

---

48. For instance P.Lond. V 1796, from the sixth century. The same was with peasants in Gaul, cf.Salvian, *De gub.dei V 38.*

BARBARIANS
ON ROMAN TERRITORY:
FROM *DEDITICII TO* DEPENDENT *COLONI*

Barbarians from regions beyond the borders who were settled on Roman territory are the only people known to have been made dependent *coloni* by means of an emperor's order, and to have come into this status not as individuals but as a group. This status improved their position as prisoners of war. The process, recorded very early in the Roman state, was only formally enacted in 409 A.D. by a law regulating the status of immigrant Scyri.

The settlement of barbarians as *coloni* on the Roman territory was not a humanitarian gesture. The Roman state was ensuring a work force on the land and tax payers for the state, *ad praestanda tributa*, as is pointed out in the well-known inscription of Plautius Silvanus at the time of Emperor Nero.[1] It was usually those defeated in war who were brought in as settlers, but there were also groups who, because of famine or power struggles within their tribes, sought the emperor's permission to settle in the Roman state, promising to pay *tributa* and to be subject to Roman laws and imperial edicts. Roman laws regulating the status of freemen and the limits of personal freedom could not be applied to those people, however: they were foreigners and *dediticii* and their freedom was at the emperor's discretion.

The Scyri of 409 A.D. were not the first conquered tribe to be reduced to the status of dependent *coloni* on Roman land. The evolution of this process dates back to Emperor Marcus Aurelius. Barbarians who moved from one side of the border in earlier centuries, differed little from the provincial peregrine population on the other. The land on which they worked and paid tax, at least initially, did not belong to them, as was also the case among the provincial population at the beginning of the Roman rule. The extension of Roman citizenship to all free people in the Empire, however, created a difference: privileges could not be accorded to those whose origin lay beyond the boundaries of the Roman state.

The law concerning Scyri and other information on the

---

1. CIL XIV 3608 (Dessau,ILS 986: ..*in qua* (sc.Moesia) *plura quam centum mill. ex numero Transdanuvianor. ad praestanda tribute cum coniugib. ac liberis et principibus aut regibus transduxit.* For settlement of barbarian groups on Roman territory in the time of Principate, see R. McMullen, *Barbarian Enclaves in the Northern Roman Empire*, Ant. class. 32/(1963):552ff.

settlement of barbarians on Roman land explains why researches of
the nineteenth century linked this to the appearance of the dependent
colonate in the Roman state. While tracing the roots of the colonate,
Huschke and Zumpt came to the conclusion that this was a phenomenon foreign to Roman society and must have originated from the
similar institutions in Gallic or German countries.[2] Zumpt considered that the legal model of the dependent *colonus*, as defined by
Savigny,[3] corresponds primarily to the position of barbarian settlers;
the colonate in Roman society would thus be the result of imperial
legislation regulating the status of the foreign, German element, in the
state. Léotard explains the quasi-slave position of the *colonus* as having been created for prisoners of war settled on Roman territory. He
restricts this, however, to groups of barbarians who arrived as *dediticii* in the Roman state. The rest, as *foederati, gentiles* and *laeti* were
in a more favorable position. *Dediticii,* he thinks, took up position
of the once free *coloni,* but since they belonged to tribes defeated in
war, their status was closer to that of slaves than of freemen. They
retained personal freedom even in the Roman state, but were
peregrine and subject to Roman authorities.[4] Like other scholars of
this time, Léotard, too, considers that the time of the Emperor
Constantine was a turning point in the development of the colonate:
from then on, the colonate relationship, regulated by custom, became
a matter of laws. Constantine would have distributed barbarians, who
had by then been moved into the imperial domain and were therefore
without a *dominus,* between cities on the one hand and private
landlords on the other; the former became *coloni publici* and as such
vicis adscripti, while the others were *coloni adscripticii.*[5]

   According to a theory by O. Seeck,[6] barbarians settled in the
Roman state, first by Marcus Aurelius and later by other emperors,
should be considered *inquilini.* The Germanic institution of *liti*

---

2. The law *De Scyris,* C.Th. V,6,3, discovered in 1823, revived the discussion,
originated by Gothofredus, of the foreign origin of the Roman colonate. See for
instance, C.P.E. Huschke, *Über den census und die Steuerverfassung der frühern
römischen Kaiserzeit,* Berlin (1847), 145ff.; U.W. Zumpt, *Über die Entstehung und
historischen Entwicklung des Colonates,* Rhein.Mus. N.F.3, (1845), Iff.

3. Savigny, *Vermischte Schriften* 2, 1ff.

4. E. Léotard, "Essai sur la condition des barbares établis dans l'Empire romain,"
(Thèse), (1983): 42ff., especially 59ff.

5. In Zumpt's opinion, op. cit., 22, the reign of Constantine was pivotal in solid-
ifying the Roman official attitude toward barbarians accepted into the Roman state:
under this emperor they were for the first time distributed among the cities and in
this way they become *vicis adscripti,* the category mentioned in the law *De Scyris.*

6. O. Seeck, *Der Untergang I,*582ff. and *RE* IV,1901, s.v. Colonatus.

provides an example of this. Although prisoners of war by origin, among the Germans the *liti* were considered freemen who worked in the fields of their masters. As they were obliged to pay him part of the yield from the land in crops or in cattle, the true position of the *liti* actually approached that of small lessee. The original unrestricted right of the master to dispose of them as he wished was reduced by an act of manumission (*Freilassung*), allowing them to acquire the basic rights of free people. With the master's permission they might enter into contracts or marriage. They still, however, had to remain on the land and to pay part of the field products to the proprietor and *patronus* as formerly.

Clausing, in his well-known review and critique of earlier theories on the origin of the Roman colonate, bases his argument on the belief that barbarians as *dediticii* became *coloni* only when the state began to distribute them individually to estate owners, and this was first done with Scyri in 409 A.D. Clausing finds no indications in the abundant data in the sources on the colonizing of barbarian tribes prior to this that would confirm that they held the status of *coloni*. The difference between tribes brought on the Roman soil as settlers before the fifth century and the Scyri in the Code was that the law of 409 A.D. solved the question of the position of individuals and their relation to the landlord. Prior to this there were only groups or tribes who moved into Roman territory on condition that they paid taxes and provided soldiers. They were then accorded the same status as the inhabitants of the newly conquered countries.[7]

Clausing quite rightly does not link the origin of the colonate as an institution to the settling of German and other tribes on the Roman soil. They merely joined an existing class which have had its own line of development in the Roman state. However, his conclusion that the emperor did not allow the settlement of barbarians with *coloni* status until the early fifth century seems less justified. Among accounts of the settling of conquered tribes or those who were *in fidem recepti* are some that indicate and others that explicitly emphasize that this procedure had been applied earlier with groups of barbarians defeated in war.

Earlier data on admission of defeated barbarians into the Roman state provide no explicit evidence on the formal side of the problem; taken altogether, however, it enables us to observe a process in imperial policy toward immigrant tribes from the second to the fifth century. A review of these data could show the main changes in this process during the centuries. To begin with the time of Marcus

---

7. Clausing, *Colonate*, 73ff.

Aurelius:

Dio Cassius gives a brief statement on the colonizing of Quadi and Marcommani defeated in the war by Marcus Aurelius: καὶ αὐτῶν οἱ μὲν ἐστρατεύσαντο ἄλλοσέ ποι πεμφθέντες... οἱ δὲ καὶ τὴν γῆν οἱ μὲν ἐν Δακίᾳ οἱ δὲ ἐν Παννονίᾳ οἱ δὲ Μυσίᾳ καὶ Γερμανίᾳ τῆ τε' Ἰταλιᾳ αὐτῆ ἔλαβον. According to evidence in HA on this same event, Marcus Aurelius settled the defeated barbarians in Italy.[8]

Information on the settling of barbarians on Roman territory may also be found in the lives of Claudius Gothicus, Aurelianus and Probus. Claudius' biographer mentions the Goths settled as *coloni* in the Roman provinces:

> *Pugnatum est enim apud Moesos et multa proelia fuerunt apud Marcianopolim. Multi naufragio perierunt, plerique capti reges, captae diversorum gentium nobiles femina < e >, impletae barbaris servis Scythi < ci > sque cultoribus Roman < a > e provinciae Factus limitis barbari colonus e Gotho. Nec ulla fuit regio quae Gothorum servum triumpali quodam servitio non haberet.*[9]

The life of Emperor Aurelianus contains information on conquered barbarians given to landowners in Etruria in Italy and regions around Alpes Maritimae:

> *Etruriae per Aureliam usque ad Alpes maritimas ingentes agri sunt hique fertiles ac silvosi. Statuerat igitur dominis, locorum incultorum qui tamen vellent gratis dare atque illic familias captivas constituere, vitibus montes conserere atque ex eo < o > per < e > vinum dare ut nihil reditum fisci acciperet, sed totum p.R. concederet.*[10]

The biography of Emperor Probus speaks of barbarians who tilled the land of senators, quoted in an alleged letter to the Senate: *Subacta est omnis qua tenditur late Germania, novem reges gentium diversarum ad meos pedes, immo ad vestros, supplices stratique iacuerunt. Omnes iam barbarii vobis arant vobis iam servunt et contra interiores gentes militant.*[11]

Data in HA contain some significant details, such as *servi barbarici Scythicique cultores* or *factus colonus a Gotho* in the Life of

8. Dio Cass. LXXII 11,4; HA, *Vita Marci* 22: *Acceptisque in deditionem Marcomanis plurimis in Italiam traduictis.* Cf. also c.24.

9. HA, *Vita Claudii*, 9, 4.

10. HA, *Vita Aurel.*48

11. HA, *Vita Probi*, 15,2.

Emperor Claudius, barbarians as *coloni* on the fields given to senators in the *Vita Aureliani.* The problem is, however, how much of this may be believed and whether it can be linked to the emperors in question.[12]

Parallel information on the colonizing of defeated peoples on Roman soil under Claudius and Probus may be found also in Zosimus. As far as Claudius is concerned, he states briefly that Goths who survived the plague in Macedonia and Thrace were either sent into the Roman army or were settled as agricultural laborers: Ὅσοι δὲ διεσώθησαν ἤ τάγματι Ῥωμαίων συνηριθμήθησαν ἤ γῆν λαβόντες εἰς γεωργίαν ταύτῃ προσεκαρτέρησαν.[13] For Probus Zosimos states that Bastarnae were allowed by him to live in Thrace subject to Roman laws: Βαστάρνας δὲ, Σκυθικὸν ἔθνος, ὑποπεσόντας αὐτῷ προσέμενος κατῴκισθε Θρᾳκίοις χωρίοις καὶ διετέλεσαν τοῖς Ῥωμαίων βιοτεύοντες νόμοις.[14]

Data from *Vita Claudii* 9,4 have not excited much attention among contemporary interpretors of this emperor's life. Damerau briefly concludes that the statement may be given credence since Zosimus speaks of the same event.[15] Probus' letter to the Senate in HA, which deals with barbarian prisoners of war cultivating land belonging to senators, is considered to be a fourth-century forgery.[16] The same information is to be found in Zosimus, albeit in a different context, thus authenticating it for the time of Probus, regardless of whether or not the letter to the senate is authentic. Authors of imperial biographies and Zosimus may have had the same sources,[17] but while Zosimus brings simple information, the emperor's biographer give it literary treatment.

The account in HA that Aurelianus distributed prisoners of war to those who had undertaken to cultivate abandoned land in northern Italy and Etruria is not recorded by any other author. Considered by itself, it is not unlikely. Its significance, regardless of

---

12. This is not the place to discuss the *Historia Augusta* problem. For this see *Historia Augusta-Colloquium* I sq., 1963 and subsequent years and R. Syme, *Emperors and Biography, Studies in the Historia Augusta,* 1971. For the value of the data quoted here, see further, notes 15 and 16.

13. Zosim, I 46, 2.

14. Zosim, I 71.

15. P. Damerau, "Kaiser Claudius Gothicus," *Klio Beiheft* 33 (1984): 73.

16. For instance E. Demougeot, *La formation de l'Europe* I, 541. The settlement of Bastarnae is considered a successful event, J.H.E. Crees, *The Reign of the Emperor Probus*, (1965): Ed. Anast., 140.

17. Cf.F. Paschoud, *Zosime, Histoire nouvelle,* text with a French translation and commentary, I 1871,159, note 70 considers Dexippus and his *Scythica* as a source for the later authors.

the time to which it refers, lies in its revealing one of the ways of using barbarian *dediticii*: uncultivated land—imperial domain? *Ager publicus?*—was distributed to those Roman citizens who were prepared to till it; in addition the state also gave them barbarian captives to use as a work force. This procedure was not unknown in previous times: during Trajan's reign, Dio Chysostomos proposed to the emperor to revive agriculture on abandoned land in the same manner;[18] according to Herodianus, Emperor Pertinax did the same with land in Italy. [19]It is possible that even Marcus Aurelius distributed the captive barbarians to landowners in Italy who were ready to take and cultivate abandoned land.

The *domini* in the passage quoted from the *Life* of Aurelianus were most probably lessees of state or imperial land. They were obliged to pay taxes either as part of their annual yield or in cash.

From the time of Diocletian, to a greater extent than earlier, barbarians migrating to Roman territory solved the problem of a work force for uncultivated land, which thus became liable to taxation. Constantius I, his co-regent, carried out a large-scale transfer of peoples from over the border to Roman land, a deed obviously considered of great merit, frequently referred to by a panegyrist of 287 ʹA.D., who points out, first, the great number of migrating tribes, *"Tot postea virtute vestra partae victoriae, tot excisae undique barbarae nationes, tot translati sint in Romana cultores, prolati limites, tot provinciae restitutae..."*; second, that these tribes were moved along with their families and properties:

> *Sed neque illae fraudes locorum nec quae plura inerant perfugia silvarum barbaros tegere potuerunt quominus dicioni tuae divinitatis omnes sese dedere cogerentur et cum coniugibus ac liberis ceteroque examine necessitudinum ac rerum suarum ad loca olim deserta transirunt ut, quae fortasse ipsi quondam depraedando vastaverant, cultu redderent serviendo.*[20]

This panegyric is the first to date the distribution of *dediticii* to landlords to work in their fields as *coloni* and to contribute to the payment of annona:

---

18. Dio Chrys.Or. VII 34.

19. Herodian. II 4,6. Herodian's statement that the emperor Pertinax distributed land in Italy to be cultivated and taxed is considered a forgery in modern historiography, because before Diocletian only provincial land was taxed. However, it may not necessarily be a forgery; the payment in question could be a state issue.

20. *Incerti Panegryicus Constatio dictus*, ed. E.Galetier, *Panegyriques latins* "Belles lettres" (1949): IV, c.1, p. 82ff.; c.8, p. 88f.

*Totis porticibus civitatum sedere captiva agmina barbarorum, viros
attonita feritate trepidantes... vinculis copulatos pueros ac puellas
familiari murmure blandientes atque hos omnes provincialibus
vestris ad obsequium distributes, donec ad destinatos sibi cultus
solitudinem ducerentur...Arat ergo nunc mihi Chamavus et
Frisius et ille vagus, ille praedator exercitio squalidi ruris operatur
et frequentat nundinas meas pecore venali et cultor barbarus laxat
annonam. Quin etfam si ad dilectu vocetur accurit et obsequiis
teritur et tergo cohercetur et servire se militiae nomine gratulatur.*[21]

Finally, in IV, 21, the panegyrist points to the difference in
approach between Diocletian and his co-regents: while the former
moved *incolae* from Asia to uncultivated fields in Thrace, the latter
brought tribes such as the Laeti and Franks, from over the border on
the land formerly belonging to the Trevirs and Nervii and settled
barbarian farmers on land of the Ambiani, Bellovaci, Tricassini and
Lingones but now laid waste:

*Itaque sicuti pridem tuo, Diocletiane Auguste, iussu deserta
Thraciae translatis incolis Asia comlpevit, sicut postea tuo, Maxi-
miane Auguste, nutu Nerviorum et Trevirorum arva iacentia
Laetus postliminio restitutus et receptus in leges Francus excoluit, ita
nunc per victorias tuas, Constanti Caesar invicte, quidquid
infrequens Ambiano et Bellovaco et Tricassino solo Lingonicoque
restabat, barbaro cultore revirescit.*

Diocletian, therefore, moved part of the population from
overcrowded regions of the Empire like Asia Minor into others that
had been laid waste because of their exposure to frequent attacks from
tribes living on the northern bank of the Danube. The problem of
who the Laeti were and whether this passage refers to one or several
categories of migrants, may be put aside here; what is important to
emphasize is that the aim was always the same: to supply *cultores* for
abandoned or uncultivated land.[22]

The manner in which Diocletian's co-regent moved and settled
barbarians on fallow Roman land, primarily in border areas, may in
some cases represent a new procedure. If the information contained
in the panegyrist is anything to judge by, the practice was widespread

---

21. Ibid., IV 9,p.89.

22. For the problem of *laeti*, see Léotard, op. cit. in note 4; E. Demougeot, *A propos
des lètes gaulois du IV siècle*, Festschrift F. Altheim II,1970,101ff. For the settlement
of barbarians on Roman territory, see her paper *Modalités d'établissement des fédérés
de Gratien et de Théodose*, Mélanges d'histoire ancienne offerte à *William Seston* (1974):
143ff.

precisely at this time. This is neglected by contemporary scholars who tend to consider Constantine's reign as a turning point in the policy of settling barbarians as *coloni* on Roman territory.[23] There is little doubt that Constantine too had recourse to this method, but the scant and mostly generalized available evidence reveals nothing new in relation to previous emperors. Like Marcus Aurelius before him, Constantine used barbarian *dediticii* or those who voluntarily moved into Roman land as soldiers or field *cultores*. According to a short passage in Zosimus, II 21,3ff., the Emperor brought back many prisoners from the war against the Sarmatians in 322 A.D.; having distributed them to the cities, he continued into Thessalonica.[24] Nothing conclusive can be drawn from this on either the objective of the measure nor on how the prisoners were utilized. Accounts of Constantine's policy toward the Sarmatians in 334 A.D. reveal no more than those on the admission of barbarians to Roman territory under Marcus Aurelius. Constantine in fact dealt with Sarmatian aristocracy defeated in a slaves' rebellion in their own country and sought refuge in the Roman state. They were admitted and settled by Constantine in Thrace, Scythia, Macedonia and Italy, according to Anonymous Valesianus.[25] According to a short account in *Vita Constantini* IV 6,2 they were allotted land to cultivate, thus exchanging barbaric savagery for Roman freedom:

Τοῖς δ'ἄλλοις τῶν πρὸς τὴν ζωὴν ἀναγκαίων εἴνεκα χώρας εἰς γεωργίαν διένεμεν ὡς ἐπὶ καλῷ τὴν συμφορὰν αὐτοῖς ὁμολογεῖν γεγενῆσθαι ῾Ρωμαικῆς ἐλευθερίας ἀντὶ βαρβάρου θηριωδίας ἀπολαύουσιν.

There was no essential difference between those defeated in war and then settled on Roman land and those who moved there voluntarily; in every case this took place thanks to the Emperor's decision, as Porphyrius Optatianus testifies, *Carm.*VII 20-22: *Indomitos reges seu pacis lubrica, victor / aut bello sternens aut mitis foedere nutu / esse tuos facis agrosque exercere tuorum.* The panegyrist in 310 A.D. lauds the merit of Constantine who transferred tribes from the farthest reaches

---

23. Zumpt, op. cit., 22; Léotard, op. cit., 43ff.

24. Zosim, II 21, 3 sq. At the same time Euseb., Vita Const. I 55. He criticizes Licinius for settling barbarians on Roman soil, in order to levy taxes: Τοιαῦτα Λικινίου αἱ διατάξεις...βαρβάρους τινὰς καὶ ἀνημέρους ἀντεισῆγε, σκήψεις ἐπινοῦν μυρίας κατὰ τῶν ὑπεκόων.

25. For this and others data, see my paper, ῾Υπήκοοι und σύμμαχοι, *Ansiedlung und Rekrutierung von Barbaren bis zum Jahr* 382, Klasisches Altertum, Spätantike und frühes Christentum, Adolf Lippold zum 65. Geburtstag gewidmet, (Würzburg 1993), 425ff.

of the Franks' land, not those once attacked by the Romans, but from their original homes, into abandoned regions of Gaul, to defend the Roman peace and cultivate the land.[26]

After Constantine, moving barbarians to Roman soil was a consistent practice of Roman emperors. Speaking of Constantius' policy towards Sarmatian tribes on Danube, Ammianus Marcellinus always stresses the Roman tendency to acquire *tributarii* who would till Roman land and regularly pay their taxes. This plays an important part in negotiations. The barbarians knew what the Romans expected of them and in some cases, although defeated in war, tried to avoid being moved to distant parts of the Empire, as for instance in 358 A.D. According to Ammianus, XVII 13,3, they agreed to the recruitment of their youth into the Roman army and to subjugation, but refused migration; however, a year later, when Roman tribunes arrived for negotiation in the country of Limigantes, these, knowing the Roman terms, showed a seeming readiness to move into Roman territory and settle in distant regions, to cultivate land and pay taxes, accepting the burden and position of *tributarii*: *Paratique intra spacia orbis Romani (si id placuerit) terras suscipere longe discretas ut diuturno otio involuti et Quietem colentes (tamquam salutarem deam) tributariorum onera subierunt et nomen.*[27]

The moving of defeated barbarians to far-flung provinces and into Italy continued into the seventies of the fourth century, under Valentinianus and Valens. Their status as *tributarii* is frequently pointed out in various sources. When Theodosius, future emperor, as *magister equitum*, defeated the Alamani in Raetium, he moved them by the emperor's order to Italy to work there on the land as *tributarii*:

> Per hanc occasionem impendio tempestivam, Alamannos gentis ante dictae metu dispersos adgressus per Raetias Theodosius ea tempestate magister equitum, pluribus caesis, quoscumque cepit ad Italiam iussu principis missit, ubi fertilibus pagis acceptis iam tributarii circumcolunt Padum.

Taifali, defeated around 377 A.D. were also moved to Italy and settled as *rura cultores* around Mutina, Regium and Parma;[28] at approximately the same time, ca. 370 A.D., Ausonius mentions Sarmatian *coloni* along the banks of the Mosella.[29]

---

26. *Panegyricus Constantino dictus VII 6.*

27. Amm.Marc. XIX 11.6.

28. Amm.Marc. XXVIII 5,15 and XXXI 9,4.

29. Auson. *Mosella 9: Arvaque Sauromatum nuper metata colonis.*

The moving of barbarians on the Roman territory was crucial to Valens' policy towards the Goths. There are various references to this in Ammianus Marcellinus, Jordanes, Orosius and Zosimus. The relationship between the Emperor and Fritigern, the leader of the Visigoths, in this respect rests on *fides* according to Ammianus: when the old *fides* was firmly established by a new document, the Goths received land for cultivation together with food, so that they might survive until the first harvest.[30] The latter condition was the same which Fritigern was to stipulate in 378 A.D., on the eve of the battle of Hadrianopolis.[31]

The account given by Jordanes contains new information: first, the envoys of the Visigoths promised to Valens that if he allowed them to settle and cultivate land in the Roman provinces of Dacia Ripensis, Moesia and Thracia, they would live in accordance with Roman laws and be obedient to his orders, *eius se legibus eiusque vivere imperiis subderentur*.[32] Second, immigrant Goths had their own *primates et duces* on Roman territory and were no longer treated as *advenae* or *peregrini: Illa namque dies Gothorum famem Romanorumque securitatem ademit, coeperuntque Gothi iam non ut advenae ac peregrini, sed ut cives et domini possessoribus imperare totasque partes septentrionales usque ad Danubium suo iure tenere.*[33]

This evidence undoubtedly reflects certain changes, above all in the attitude of barbarians whom the Romans were prepared to settle on their land. Their readiness to subjugate themselves to Roman laws and the orders of the Roman Emperor is in fact a subtle quest for equality with Roman subjects. At the same time, however, they retained their leaders; they were *advenae* and *peregrini* in the Roman state, who at one moment began to behave as if they were *cives*, on a par with those who could own land as *domini.* Zosimus, relating the same account as Jordanes in *Getica* XXV 131, conceives their request to the emperor as an offer of subjugation, not as *dediticii* but in the guise of faithful and trustworthy allies, ὑπισχνεῖσθαι τε πληρώσειν ἔργον αὐτῷ συμμάχων πιστῶν καὶ βεβαίων.[34]

It is clear from this evidence that the Goths wanted to be

---

30. Amm. Marc.XXXI 4,8: *Nam postquam innumerae gentium multitudines, per provincias circumfusae, pandentesque se in spatia ampla camporum, regiones omnes et cuncta opplevere montium iuga, fides quoque vetustatis recenti documento firmata est. Et primus cum Almavivo suscipitur Fritigernus quibus et alimenta pro tempore et subigendos agros tribui statuerat imperator.*

31. Amm. Marc. XXXI 12,8.

32. Jord., *Get.* XXV 131.

33. Jord., *Get.* XXVI 138.

34. Zosim IV 20,5; IV 26,1.

admitted to the Roman state not as *dediticii coloni*, but as free citizens, *cives*. They were not, however, granted this by Valens, nor were they given the right to own the land on which they were settled. The Alani, brought in Gaul around 442 A.D. did not have this right either. In an account of their rebellion of that year, the term *domini terrae* still occurs: *Alani quibus terrae Gallicae cum incolis dividendae a patricio Aetio traditae fuerunt, resistentes armis subiegunt et expulsis dominis terrae possessionem adipiscantur.*[35]

It might be said that the Roman state also altered its attitude towards barbarians admitted to its territory. They were no longer regarded as those mentioned by panegyrists in the late third and early fourth centuries. And when—as happened towards the end of the seventies of the fourth century—Roman officers in charge of controlling the transmigration of Goths permitted to settle in the Roman provinces on Danube, abused their position to choose from among them those who would be suitable as servants or farm workers, this is condemned by Roman authors.[36]

Abuses by Roman officers led to a rebellion of Goths, one which ended in a crushing defeat of the Roman army at Hadrianopolis in 378 A.D. Having defeated the Romans, the Goths colonized Thrace and Dacia Ripensis as if these provinces were their native country, as Jordanis notes: *quo tempore Vesegothae Thracias Daciaque Ripense post tanti gloria tropaei tamquam solum genitalem coeperunt incolere.*[37] Evidence is lacking on how the Roman authorities reacted to this arbitrary settlement of Goths along the probably deserted border area and on whether the settled barbarians were incorporated into the fiscal system as *capita* on imperial or public land or as landowners.

The wish of the Goths to be received into the Roman state not only as *tributarii* and *dediticii*, but as subjects, on equal terms with the old provincial population, seems to be officially granted for the first time by a contract dating from 382 A.D. The agreement between Theodosius and the Goths provoked a lively reaction among the Roman public. The contemporary opinions were divided in interpreting this event: Synesius from Cyrene, a panegyrist and rhetorician, attacks the Emperor's decision: he had admitted barbarians defeated in war as allies and considered them worthy of Roman citizenship; he

35. *Chron, Gall.* 127 (MGH AA IX 660) ad a. 442.

36. Zosim IV 20,6: διαβάντων μὲν ἐφ'ᾧτε ὅπλων δίχα τοὺς βαρβάρους ἐπὶ τὰ 'Ρωμαίων ὅρια παραπέμψαι μεδενὸς δὲ γενομένων ἑτέρου πλὴν γυναικῶν εὐπροσώπων ἐπιλογῆς καὶ παίδων ὡραίων εἰς αἰσχρότητα θήρας ἢ οἰκετῶν ἢ γεωργῶν κτήσεως.

37. Jord. *Get.* XXVI 138.

had given them gifts and although old and mortal enemies, had given land in the Roman state: ὁ δὲ τῷ πολεμῳ νικῶν ἐλεῳ παρὰ πλεῖστον ἡττᾶτο καὶ ἀνίστη τῆς ἱκετείας καὶ συμμάχους ἐποίει καὶ πολιτείας ἠξίου καὶ μετεδίδου γερῶν καὶ γῆς τι ἐδάσατο τοῖς παλαμναίοις Ῥωμαικῆς.[38] In contrast to him, another orator of the time, Themistius, defended and exonerated the Emperor's action, pointing out the advantage to the Roman state. He gives analogies in past Roman history: in the same manner Galatians had at one time been settled as foreigners in Asia Minor and Roman military commanders Lucullus and Pompeius and even Augustus, who had waged wars against them, had not destroyed them, but included them into the Roman state. Now Galatians were no longer referred to as barbarians, but were considered Roman: they took part in wars on an equal footing, paid taxes and were subject to the same laws as Roman citizens: τοὔνομα γὰρ αὐτοῖς τὸ πάλαι παραμε Μένηκεν, ὁ βίος δὲ σύμφυλος ἤδη. καὶ εἰσφέρουσιν ἅς ἡμεῖς εἰσφορὰς καὶ στρατευονται ἅς ἡμεῖς στρατίας καὶ ἄρχοντας δέχονται ἐξ ἴσου τοῖς ἄλλοις καὶ νόμοις τοῖς αὐτοῖς ὑπακούουσιν. "And so it is now with the *Scythians*," Themistius goes on, "after the recent conflict with them; they have become those who together with us offer sacrifice, sit at table with us and wage war together with us and together bear the burden of taxes: οὕτω καὶ Σκύθας ὀψόμεθα ὀλίγου χρόνου. νῦν μὲν γὰρ ἔτι τὰ προσκρούσματα αὐτῶν νέα ληψόμεθα δ᾽ οὖν οὔκ εἰς μακρὰν ὁμοσπόνδους, ὁμοτραπέζους, ὁμοῦ στρατευομένους, ὁμοῦ λειτουργοῦντας.[39] The terms ὁμόσπονδοι and ὁμοτραπέζοι may be rhetorical here, and taken from the ancient Greek authors;[40] the formulation ὁμοῦ λειτουργοῦντες merits particular attention, as it obviously refers to the payment of taxes. This corresponds to somewhat different wording for the Galatians, εἰσφέρουσι ἅς ἡμεῖς εἰσφορὰς. It is clear that the Goths were admitted in the Roman state under more favorable conditions than had been the case with barbarians hitherto. Zosimos reports that Theodosius at the

---

38. Synes. Περὶ Βασιλείας, XXI. Cf. for this L. Schmidt, *Die Ostgermanen* (Nach-druck 1969) 419 f.; A. Piganiol, *L'empire chrétien*, (1972), 235; E. Stein, *Bas-Empire* I" 194; A. Lippold, *Theodosius der Grosse und seine Zeit*, 1968, 26f. and idem, *RE Suppl;.* XIII, 1973, 861f.; E. Demougeot, *Modalités d'établissement des fédérés barbares de Gratien à Théodose, Mélanges d'histoire offert à William Seston*, 1974, 143f. M. Cesa, *Romani e barbari sul Danubio*, Studi Urbinati 57, 1984, 80 ff.; F.M. Ausbüttel, "Die Dedition des Westgothen von 382 und ihre historische Bedeutung," *Athenaeum* 66 (1988): 604 ff.

39. Themist. *Or.* XVI 211 d.

40. Herod. IX 16; Diarch.I 24.

outset of his reign received some barbarians as friends and as those who would wage war together with him.[41] This account is complemented by a fragment from Eunapius which says that Theodosius handed over Thrace to the barbarians.[42] Two groups of Goths appear in Jordanes: the Emperor Gratianus negotiated and concluded an alliance with those led by Alatheus and Saphrac, ceding them *pacemque victualia* and land in Pannonia; the Goths who followed Athanaricus, became Roman *foederati* after his sudden death in Constantinople, and, as it seems, remained on the Roman soil. Eunapius' account of their having been given Thrace would seem to apply to the latter. Jordanes, however, does not consider this an innovation of Theodosius, citing a contract with the Goths, which Constantine had once concluded with them, and was now renewed.[43]

References by orators at the time of Theodosius on the one hand and by Zosimus and Jordanes on the other, have little in common. It is clear that the account in Zosimus is stereotypical. Possibly, Jordanes, when he says that Goths under Athanaricus became Roman *foederati*, is simplifying or adapting the terminology of his own time to an act of Theodosius by which barbarians who settled on Roman territory were equated with Roman subjects when it came to their obligations to the state.

Theodosius' treatment of the Goths who were admitted into the Roman state in 382 A.D., whether it had a precedent or not—Jordanes mentions renewal of a contract from Constantine's time—drew the attention of his contemporaries who reacted in various ways. It did not, however, become a keystone in his later policy towards barbarians. In 386 A.D. he settled Ostrogoths, together with Grutungi, defeated on the Danube, to cultivate the fields in Phrygia, as Claudius Claudianus testifies, *In Eutrop. II 153: Ostrogothis colitur mixtisque Gruthungis / Phryx ager.* Though defeated in war, they too received some rights, *iura quibus victis dedimus*, says the same poet, *In Eutrop. II 576.* In time of war they were to be recruited into the Roman army.[44] Settled on Roman land as freemen with certain rights, they were considered *coloni* and *advenae*.[45]

---

41. Zosim. IV 56.

42. Eunap. *Fr.*, FHG IV, ed. Muller, p. 36.

43. Jord., *Get.* XXVI; XXVIII.

44. For settlement of Grutungi in Phrygia, see Seeck, Untergang V, 306. They were settled as captives, see Cons.Const.,Chron.Min. I 244: *victi atque expugnati et in Romania captivi adducti gens Greuthenorum a nostris Theodosio et Arcadio;* cf. also Zosim V 13: Claud. *In Eutrop.*II 183; Socrat.HE XI 8; Sozom. HE VIII 4,2.

45. Cf. Chron. Gall. s.a. 442; Paul.Pelens. GSEL L 16,1.

For many centuries the settlement of tribes or groups of barbarians on Roman soil had fiscal objectives, as clearly stated in several sources, as well as others, such as obtaining recruits for the army or workers in the mines. The status of immigrants evolved in time from the *dediticii* of the first or second century to those who were subject to Roman law and equated with the population of the province in which they were colonized—at least as far as recruitment and taxation were concerned. Both before and after Theodosius, they were *cultores* or *rura cultores*, people who tilled the land, or *tributarii*, as they were enrolled as *capita* in the tax-rolls. The term *colonus* seldom occurs in sources on the transmigration of the barbarian tribes outside the Empire. These were actually considered *advenae* working as *coloni*, therefore *loco colonorum,* as those who possessed neither land nor property. They were then in the position of dependent *coloni* or *adscripticii*. The Roman state guaranteed them this status by law, as is shown by the edict on Scyri of 409 A.D., C.Th. V 6,3. This text is the only unambiguous evidence of the conditions under which barbarians defeated in war might be used in the fields on Roman territory: all landowners were allowed to take them on to their estates, but on condition that they were to be used only as *coloni:*

Ideoque damus omnibus copiam ex praedicto genere hominum agros proprios frequentandi, ita ut omnes sciant susceptos non alio iure quam colonatus apud se futuros.

Further reading of the passage makes clear that Scyri distributed among landowners were considered *coloni* who were *adscripticii* and registered in the tax-rolls as *capita* on a certain estate and it was forbidden that anyone else should take them on their land. If they did, the law provided the same penalty as for other fugitive *coloni:*

Nullique licere ex hoc genere colonorum ab eo cui semel adtributi fuerint, vel fraude aliquem adducere vel fugientem suscipere, poena proposita, quae recipientes alienis censibus adscribtos vel non proprios colones insequitur.

Though these were people taken captive in war, no one had the right to use them as slaves in his urban service, thus depriving the state of a tax payer; landowners could avail of their labor only as that of freemen:

Opera autem eorum terrarum domini libera utantur ac nullus sub acta peraequatione vel censui ... acent nullique liceat velut donatos eos a iure census in servitutem trahere urbanisque obsequiis addicere.

This last regulation was of crucial importance for the state and may be compared with laws referring to other *adscripticii.* Since they were used as *coloni*, these former barbarians had to remain on the land where they were sent and where the landlord registered them as *coloni* on his estate.[46]

One might ask whether the law on Scyri was aimed at solving their position, or was it only an application of an existing regulation to one particular case. Was the custom to take barbarians as *coloni adscripticii* an established practice or was it introduced after Theodosius? One might also ask whether in future this custom is to be the only way of using barbarian *dediticii* in Roman agriculture.

The premise that a similar practice of settling barbarians existed before the fifth century seems worth defending. The distribution of captive barbarians to landowners is indisputably confirmed as early as Diocletian's reign, in the Panegyric to Constantius I in 287 A.D.; the *Life* of Aurelianus in HA probably also treats the same practice. But at that time there were probably no strict regulations forbidding the use of barbarian *dediticii* in any other status, but that of dependent *coloni.*

In the seventh decade of the fourth century, migrant barbarians were already called *tributarii*.[47] This term was used from Constantine's time onward for dependent categories of *coloni*, particularly in what concerned the fiscal aspect of their dependence.[48] *Tributarius* is interchangeable with the terms *colonus iuris alieni* or *adscripticius*. In contrast to the *tributarius* is the *liber plebeius* who may not leave the place where he is enrolled in the tax-rolls, but be is not dependent on the landowner, because he himself pays his taxes. Barbarians on Roman territory could be *tributarii* and *adscripticii*, but not *liberi plebei*, because they were foreigners (*advenae*) and did not have their own land; in the tax-rolls in the Roman state therefore they were *capita* on another's land and not *possessores.*

The distribution of barbarian *dediticii* to the landlords in the Roman state was probably not the only way in which they arrived in the Roman fields as *cultores* or *coloni*. Settling them on imperial or state land continued to retain its importance. The Ostrogoths and Grutungi of 396 A.D. were probably *coloni* on the emperor's domain

---

46. Further sections of this law concern an interdiction on settling barbarians in Thrace and Illyricum, probably in order to prevent them from fleeing to their tribesmen on the north bank of the Danube.

47. Amm.Marc. XIX 11,6; XXVIII 5,5; XXVII 13,4. The others attested terms are vague, as cultores (Eumen, *Panegiricus Constantio Caesari*, Pan.lat. IV 1, IV 21; XII 22,3) or *rura cultores* (Amm.Marc.XXXI 9,4) and *incola* (Jord. XXII 15 and Pan.lat. IV 21).

48. Jones, *LRE* II 799: "The word *tributarius* is sometimes used to denote a *colonus* for whose taxes the landlord is liable"; see also Eibach, Kolonat, 222: "Tributarius is ein Mann der aug Gut eines Grundherren arbeitet und seine Steuer zahlt." See Segrè, *Colonate,* 105 who dates the origin of this term in the time of Diocletian's fiscal reform.

in Phrygia and not distributed to individual proprietors.

When distributing barbarians as *coloni* to the landowners, the Roman state gave the *dominus fundi* the right to retain them on his land; in cases where they were sent to the cities, as for instance in the seventies or nineties of the fourth century, the state controlled them through its *rectores*.[49] Their freedom was restricted in both cases, which is why groups of barbarians tended to settle on Roman land in the status of those subjugated to Roman laws.[50] They also worked towards rising from *colonus* status to that of landlords. Two examples are known of an attempt to drive the landowners out by force: at the time of Emperor Valens, Goths on the Danube began to behave like *cives* and *domini*, suppressing those who were *possessores*[51] and in 442 A.D. Alani in Gaul drove out the owners of the land on which they were settled and seized it for themselves.[52]

---

49. Amm Marc. XXXI 16,8. It is possible that the position of a *rector* of the Goths in Phrygia held Tribigild, see Zosim V 13.

50. Cf. Jord. Get. XXV 131; Zosim I 71: Τοῖς ʻΡωμαίων βιοτεύοντες νόμοις.

51. Jord., *Get*. XXVI 137: *illa namque dies Gothorum famem Romanorumque securitatem ademit, coeperuntque Gothi iam non ut advenae et peregrini, sed ut cives et domini possessoribus imperare totasque partes septentrionales usque ad Danubium suo iure tenere.*

52. Chron. Gall. s.a.442.

INQUILINI:
PEOPLE WITHOUT DOMICILE (*SEDES*) LOST DIGNITY

According to O. Seeck's (1901) theory, barbarians first settled on Roman territory by Marcus Aurelius and later by other emperors, should be considered *inquilini*.[1] This was one of the categories whose freedom was reduced in the Early Empire, judging by some laws in the *Digesta*. Seeck sums up the position of the *inquilini* as follows: they were freemen who could marry and even be *tutores*. On the other hand, they were in the personal possession (*in persönlichen Eigentum*) of the landowner, who was bound to register them as property in his *census* record (*Dig. L* 15,4,8). They could be bequeathed in someone's will, but not without *praedia quibus adhaerent*.[2]

Inquilini were evidently a separate category of people between slavery and freedom because the term remained parallel to *coloni*, until the Later Empire. It is difficult to define the peculiar feature of their position, however, especially in the Later Empire, since in legal texts where they are found together with other groups of semi-dependent people they obviously share a number of traits, particularly in what concerns the payment of tax. The same regulations applied to them as to the *adscripticii* in C.J.XI 48,6, as well as to *adscripticii* and *servi* in C.J. III 38,11 (334 A.D.), to *coloni* in general in C.J.XI 53,1 (370 A.D.) or those envisaged for *tributarii* in C.J.XI 48,2 (Arcadius and Honorius) and C.Th X 12,2 (370 A.D.); they were treated in the same way as *coloni originarii* and *originales* in C.Th.V 18,1 (419 A.D.), as *coloni originarii* and *servi* in Nov.Valent. XXVII 4 (449 A.D.) and Nov.Valent. XXXV 3 (452 A.D.); the law of A.D.442, C.J. III 26,11 applies to *inquilini* and *servi*. With some authors of the fourth and fifth century, *inquilinus* appear in contexts where the term could easily be replaced by the term *colonus*.

The similarity of the position of *inquilinus* and *colonus* in relation to the state and taxation and the use of the term *inquilinus* in literary sources gave rise to a conviction among some contemporary scholars that there was no distinction between them and that *inquilinus* was in fact a *colonus* who had not been entered in the *census* lists.[3] Some scholars consider that the terms *colonus* and *inquilinus* were

---

1. Seeck, "Untergang," I 582ff. *RE* IV, (1901): 496.

2. *Dig.* XXX 1.112.

3. Fustel de Coulanges, *Colonat*, 99f.; Collinet, *Colonat*, 96.

synonymous;[4] and others believe that the difference between *inqui-linus* and *colonus* cannot be determined, at least insofar as legal texts are concerned.[5]

In the Early Roman Empire *coloni* and *inquilini* occur together, in the *Digesta* and on inscriptions, as those from Henchir Metich in North Africa.[6] Legal texts in the *Digesta* differentiate between the two: *coloni* are tenants on another's land, while *inquilini* are tenants of another's house. [7]A.H.M. Jones maintains that this difference may have extended into the Later Roman Empire and notes that even if *colonus* and *inquilinus* were not synonymous, they were almost identical.[8]

There is little doubt that the *inquilini* who worked on another's land were similar in their position to the *coloni*. The law of the time treated them as *coloni adscripticii*. Like them they were, according to a law of 371 A.D., C.J.XI 53,1, tied to the land *nomine et titulo colonorum*. What they had in common with other groups of semi-dependents working on another's land can be ascertained from legal texts which contain references to them. These show the differences between them and which group they most resembled:

• As both *tributarii* and *servi*, *inquilini* were bound to a certain *dominus*, C.J.XI 48,12 (396 A.D.): *servos vel tributarios vel inquilinos apud dominos volumus remanere;*

• As *censiti*, *inquilini* could not leave the place where they were registered in the tax-rolls. If they did, as with *adscripticii* in the law C.J.XI 48,6 (366 A.D.), they would be considered fugitives and the provincial governor was responsible for returning them.[9]

---

4. Clausing, *Colonate*, 17 f. n. 3. See A.H.M. Jones, LRE 799: "The term *inquilinus* is also not infrequently used but is apparently synonymous with *colonus*, probably denoting a man domiciled on an estate but not a lessee of land, a cottager who worked as a laborer or craftsman." But he admits, quoting the law of 396, that at the end of the fourth century, "their condition appears to be indistinguishable and almost identical" (ibid.).

5. Eibach, *Kolonat*, 243: "Damit aber bleibt die Frage einer möglichen Abgrenzung zu anderen Begriffen innerhalb der Terminologie des Kolonats immer noch offen; auch das Problem zeitlicher und regionaler Unterschiede ist nicht gelöst."

6. For example *Dig.* XIX 2,21; 24, 1; XLI 2,37; XLIII 32, 1,1: L 15,4,8; Cf. Also VII 8,2ff.; XIX 1.30; 2,21. - The inscription from Henchir Metich: CIL VIII 29902 (FIRA n.114) and others, see J. Colendo, *Le colonat en Afrique sous le Haut-Empire*, 1977; D. Flach, *Chiron* 8, (1978), 441ff. As παροίκοι together with γεωργοί, they are documented in the inscriptions, see Dittenberger, *Syll.Orint.* N. 519.

7. *Dig.* XIX 2,25; XLIII 32; Svet. Nero 44.

8. See above, n.4.

9. Eibach, *Kolonat*, 234 links *adscripticius* in this law with *inquilinus* and thinks that the sentence *ubi censiti atque educati natique sunt* reveals a fine distinction between

• If the *capitatio* was abolished, *inquilini*, like *coloni adscripticii*, according to the law of A.D.371 on Illyrian *coloni*, C.J.XI 53,1 did not attain the right to go where they wished, because it was the colonate relationship which bound them to a certain *dominus*.

• According to a law of 419 A.D., C.Th.V 18,1, *inquilini*, like *coloni*, had to remain on the land for 30 years. A similar issue occurs in Nov.Valent. XXVII 4, from 449 A.D., where the same principles prescribed by Honorius for *coloni iuris privati*[10] apply to *originarii et coloni, inquilini et servi* who were *perpetui patrimoniales emphyteuticarii et rei publicae*.

• The freedom of *inquilini* to take holy orders or to become a curial was restricted, as it was for *originarii, coloni* and *servi*: the permission of the *dominus* was required, Nov.Valent. XXXV 3 (452 A.D.).

• The law of 334, C. J III 38, 11 envisages that the *proxima agnatio* of slaves, of *coloni adscripticiae condicionis* and *inquilini*, in the case of division of the estate on which they worked, should remain together, with the same owner.[11]

In sum, the similarities between the *inquilini* and other categories of *coloni* may be reduced to the following: the *inquilinus*, like the *tributarius* or *adscripticius*, could not leave his landlord: to leave on one's own initiative was considered flight, just as it was for *colonus adscripticius*. Some *inquilini* were entered in the tax-rolls; they were *censiti*, but like the *adscripticii*, tax (*capitatio*) was not a primary consideration in binding them to the estate on which they worked and to the *dominus* to whom the land belonged.

• A.H.M. Jones's opinion that the term *inquilinus* did not change its basic meaning in the Later Empire, remaining the lessee of another's house, is likely correct. Jones adds that *inquilinus* working

---

the two categories and supposes that we have here an *inquilinus adscripticius* before us. But in note 589 on the same page he quotes Jones's opinion who in LRE, 1329, note 68, concludes that the wording in C.J.III 38,1 (A.D.334) *vel colonum adscripticiae condicionis seu inquilinum*, as well as *adscripticius* in the law C.J.XI 48,12 are Justinian's interpolation. The first mention of an *adscripticius* would be a law of A.D. 466, C.J. I 12,6. It is true that C.J.XI 48,6 does not explicitly mention *adscripticius*, but it is clear that this category is in question.

10. Nov.Valent. XXVII 4: *De originariis et colonis, inquilinis ac servis utriusque sexus, peculiis atque agnationibus designatu iuris, id est perpetui patrimonialis emphyteuticarii et rei publicae, post triginta annorum curricula nulla deinceps actio moveatur.*

11. Jones, *loc.cit.* in n.9, qualifies the term *adscripticius* in this law also as later interpolation; the same regulation refers to slaves on imperial domains in Sardinia in C.Th.III 25,1. Nevertheless, it does not prove interpolation theory in the first mentioned law, C.J.III 38,11. It could be a general rule, proscribed in C.J.III 38,11 and applied to one specific case in C.Th.II 25,1.

on the estate, as a craftsmen or an agricultural laborer, could earn his living.[12] In fact he could be tied, because of owing rent, to the house owner and had to work off his debt by laboring on the land of the same owner, together with *coloni,* tied to the land because of rent arrears. This concept of the state of *inquilini* could explain the difference between *coloni* and *inquilini* in the Later Roman Empire. In Later Roman state and laws, the *inquilinus,* who worked on the land, was important as a *caput* liable to tax, thus making the term similar in meaning to others who found themselves in the same position. Working another's land became characteristic of the *inquilini* as may be seen from the definition given by Isidore of Seville, *Orig.IX* 4,37: *Inquilini vocati quasi incolentes aliena. Non habent propriam sede , sed in terra aliena inhabitant.*

The shift in meaning, from tenant of a house to laborer on another's land, must have come about relatively early, as may be seen from some regulations contained in *Digesta,* L 15,4,8 on the ob-ligation of the landlord to register, together with his land, both *coloni* and *inquilini* who worked on it, and again in XXX 112 (Marcianus) on bequeathing *inquilini* together with the land to which they were tied. This could happen only if *inquilinus* was in debt. The basic feature of the *inquilinus* position, of not having a house of his own but living in another's, lingered, however, until the Later Empire and St. Augustine says: *Inquilini non habent propriam domum, habitant in alienas, incolae autem vel advenae, utique adventicii perhibentur.*[13]

This evidence expands the discussion to the terms *incola* and *advena.* This could be important, too, when posing the question of whether Barbarians as foreigners in the Roman state (*advenae*) were settled there with the status of *inquilini.*

Some authors of the Later Republic and the Early Empire approximate *inquilinus* to the term *advena.*[14] Augustine links the *inquilinus* with other terms as are παροίκος, *incola* and *advena* and explains the difference in the following way,

> *quod est enim in graeco paroikos atqui nostri inquilinus, aliqui incola, nonnumquam etiam advena interpretati sunt. Inquilini non habentes propriam domam habitant in alienas, incolae autem vel advenae utique adventicii perhibentur.*[15]

---

12. See above, n. 4.

13. August., *Enarr. in Psalm.* CVIII Serm.,91.

14. For *advena,* see Th. LL s.v. 827. For *advenae* and *peregrini* as opposite to *cives,* see Cic. *De orat.* I 249; *De leg. Agr.* 2,94. See Salust., *Catil.,* XXI: *M. Tullius Inquilinus civis urbis Romae.* Appian., BG II 1,f.

15. August. *Enarr. in Psalm.* CVIII, *Serm.* 91.

Isidore of Seville, in a reference to this information, *Orig.* IX 4,37, formulates the difference between these terms as follows: *Inquilini sunt qui emigrant et non perpetuo manent. Advenae autem vel incolae adventicii perhibentur, sed permanentes; et inde incolae quia iam habitatores sunt ab incolendo.*

It is clear that two categories have been confused here: strangers who came from another town or regions, i.e. who lived in places from which they did not originate (*advenae, incolae*) and those who lived as tenants in another's house or on another's estate, regardless of where they came from originally. There are, therefore, two things which are confused in the sources: a) origin (*origo*) and social status (a man who did not own his house, but lived as a tenant in another's).

Relying on the data by Sallust and Appianus, Revilout came to the conclusion that the *origo* was the crucial element defining the position of the *inquilini*, those who lived outside their homeland.[16] O. Seeck, equating the terms *inquilinus* and *incola*, concludes that Barbarians whom Roman emperors, beginning with Marcus Aurelius, settled on Roman territory, were also in this position.[17] *Origo* as a significant element in determining the meaning of the term *inquilinus* is pointed out by Saumagne: for a *colonus* the principle of being linked to his place of origin would act directly, so that, at least from the time of the Emperor Zeno, simply by virtue of birth and *origo*, he was tied to the land, i.e. he was *adscripticius*. At that time the *inquilinus* found himself in the position of the former *colonus*: *origo* prevented him from leaving the land he cultivated until he had spent thirty years on the same estate. [18]Finally, P. Rosafio in an article dated 1984, concludes that the essential difference between *colonus* and *inquilinus* was that the latter was not *originarius* of the place where he lived.[19]

It remains to consider more closely the consequences implied by the circumstance that *inquilinus* was not *originarius*. This would first of all mean that he did not originate from the estate where he worked as tenant and had not been enrolled on the tax-rolls as someone permanently domiciled here. But he was neither *advena* nor an *incola*, at least not as understood by Isidore in the text quoted above. *Origo* by itself however, did not determine social status. An *incola*, for instance, coming from another place could, according to *Digesta*, L 16, 239 A.D. have his own land, but in another town or

16. Revilout, *Note sur inquilinat*, 1861, cit. Taken from Eibach, *Kolonat*, 233, n. 585.

17. See above, note 1.

18. Cf. Saumagne, *Origo* 501 and passim.

19. P. Rosafio, *Inquilinus*, Opus 3,1984,121ff.

region. Reduced to his basic meaning, *origo* designated the place
where somebody paid tax. *Incola* had a *sedes*, apparently on the estate
where he was enrolled on the tax-lists: *qui alicuius oppidi finibus ita
agrum habent, ut in eum se quasi in aliquem sedem recipient, Dig.loc.cit.*
Therefore *inquilinus*, in contrast to *advena* and *incola*, did not stay
permanently: *Inquilini sunt qui emigrant et non perpetuo manent,* says
Isidore.

Inquilini did not always have to be foreigners. There were
circumstances in which free plebeians could be reduced to the
position of *inquilini*, or in this of *coloni*. According to a well-known
passage in Salvianus, *De gub. dei* V, some small holders, having lost
their homes and land properties because of the impossibility of paying taxes, moved onto the estates of the wealthy, thus finding
themselves in the same position as *inquilini.*

Primarily a tenant in someone else's house, who could easily
leave the place where he lived, by virtue of not being *censitus, inquilinus* became increasingly closer in position to the *colonus*, partly
because of rent due and partly because he had nowhere to go. But the
difference between him and the *colonus* remained in theory and the
legislator around A.D.400 still recognized it. But it was of no consequence where descendants were concerned, as is shown by the law
C.J.XI 48,13:

> *Definimus ut inter inquilinos colonosque, quorum quantum ad
> originem pertinet vindicandam indiscreta eademque paene videtur
> esse condicio, licet sit discrimen in nomine, suscepti liberi vel
> utroque vel neutro parents censito, statum paternae condicionis
> agnoscant.*

About 465 A.D. the difference remained only in name.

Freemen who had become *inquilini* or *coloni*, in the words of
Salvianus, *De gub. dei* V, 44 lost not only their house and land (*sedes*)
but also their dignity (*dignitas*):

> *Ac sicut solent aut hi qui hostium terrore compulsi ad castella se
> conferunt, aut hi qui perdito ingenuae incolumitatis statu ad
> asylum aliquod desperatione confugiunt, ita et isti, quia tueri
> amplius vel sedem vel dignitatem suorum natalium non queunt,
> iugo se inquilinae abiectionis addicunt, in hanc necessitatem reducti
> ut extorres non facultatis tantum, sed etiam condicionis suae atque
> exultantes non a rebus tantum suis sed etiam a se ipsis ac perdentes
> secum omnia sua et rerum proprietate careant et ius libertatis
> amittant.*[20]

---

20. "And as happens with people driven by fear of an enemy and who seek safety in

Although they had neither *sedes* nor *dignitas* and were considered the lowest social category among freemen, *inquilini* retained
their freedom longer than other similar groups, in the sense that they
could leave the house and its owner and go where they wished. This,
among other things, differentiated them from the Barbarians settled
by the emperors on Roman territory. They became similar only at the
point where *inquilini* became *tributarii* and when their position was
equated with that of *coloni*. Even Salvian does not differentiate
between *coloni* and *inquilini*. The difference quite disappeared for his
younger contemporary Sidonius Apollinaris. In his *Letter* V 19, he
refers to the descendants of *a nutrix* and *colonus* from the estates
belonging to different owners and proposes the following solution:

> *Sub condicione concedo: si stupratorem pro domino iam patronus*
> *originali solvas inquilinatu. Mulier autem illa iam libera est: quae*
> *tum demum videbitur non ludibrio seducta sed assumpta coniugio,*
> *si reus noster, pro quo precaris, mox cliens factus e tributario*
> *plebeiam potius incipiat habere personam quam colonariam.*[21]

He proposes, therefore, that the other landowner as master
should set the "guilty" *inquilinus* free from his inherited status while
the woman is free in any case. In this manner, *colonus* and *tributarius*
will become *plebeius* and *cliens*, who will pay tax by himself.

This text, at first glance imprecise, because the same person is
treated as *originalis inquilinus, colonaria persona* and *tributarius*,
reveals the real state of affairs: this is a status to which is opposed the
libera persona of the woman and a future *plebeius* who could be a
cliens. It means that a former *inquilinus*, working on the land of the
owner of the house in which he lives, has sunk to the position of a
dependent *colonus*, probably because of overdue rent; although in the
position of a *colonus*, he has not paid tax by himself, because he did
not own any land. He did not keep any part of the income from the

---

fortresses or those who have lost their free status and in their hopelessness seek
asylum somewhere, so these also, as they cannot keep either the home or the dignity
in which they were born, knowingly take on the yoke of despised inquilini, reduced
to such that they are deprived not only of property but of status, driven out not only
from their own land but alienated from their very selves, thereby losing all they
have and ceasing to exist as they were formerly, remain both without property and
without the rights of free people."

21. "I pardon the seducer if you free the defiler from the condicio of inquilinus into
which he was born. This woman is already free; ultimately, it cannot be said that she
was seduced by lust, but taken to wife and if our culprit, for whom you beg me, were
soon to become a client instead of a tributarius, he will be held in a higher esteem as
a person who is plebeius rather than one who is colonus."

land for himself, because he was repaying the rental arrears for the house in which he lived by working on the land. As a worker on another's land, he had to be entered on the owner's *professio* as a *caput*. By virtue of the fact that it was the landowner who paid taxes, this former *inquilinus* had become *tributarius*.

Tributarius therefore has a range of meanings and includes all those who paid tax through the landowner.[22] *Coloni iuris alieni* and all those who were *adscripticii*, i.e. who were not entered on the tax-rolls under their own name, could find themselves in this position. barbarians settled on the Roman territory were also *tributarii*, above all those who were distributed to landowners in the way envisaged by the law of the Scyri.

Despite its comprehensive character, the term *tributarius* is not frequently met in legal texts, certainly because it was replaced by other terms designating categories of people paying tax indirectly. There are, however, three laws where *tributarius* and *colonus* or *tributarius* and *inquilinus* occur side by side:

- C.Th. XI 7,2 (319 A.D.): *Unusquisque decurio pro ea portione conveniatur, in qua vel ipse vel colonus vel tributarius eius convenitur et colligit;*
- C.Th. X 12,2 (370 A.D.). *Si quis etiam vel tributarius repperitur vel inquilinus ostenditur, ad eum protinus redeat* cuis se esse profitetur;
- C.J.XI 48,12 (396 A.D.): *Servos vel tributaries vel inquilinos apud dominos volumus remanere.*

All three laws underline the link with the *dominus*. The first example refers to the *tributarius* but also to the *colonus* as of persons belonging to a *dominus*. In fact it emphasizes that this is a *colonus* entered in the *professio* of a landlord who was *decurio*; as far as tax liability is concerned, the *dominus terrae* was also responsible for *coloni* who worked on his land. This rule applies at the end of the Republic, as far as we can learn from Cicero's *In Verrem*, II 53.

The *inquilini* described in the other two laws, must have been people who had fallen through indebtedness into the position of *coloni*, working another's land and therefore in fiscal terms equated

---

22. A. Segrè, in his paper, "The Byzantine Colonate," *Traditio* 5, (1947): 105, devoted the following lines to this passage: "The passage presents the further difficulty that the genuine *colonus* could not have been freed by his master. But apart from this, it shows that this particular *tributarius* was an *inquilinus* of the same condition as a *colonus originarius* and that he had a master *(dominus)*; while the peasant *(plebeius rusticus)* was *cliens* of a *patronus* and a free man. If the passage of Sidonius is correct, it may be that at this time the *tributarii* (peasant *sub patrocinio*) had become *coloni*. But certainly in the texts of the fourth entury, from the time of Diocletian until the year 371 (Cod 11, 53) *tributarius* appears to refer to a free peasant who in some cases might have become *cliens* of a *patronus*."

with *coloni* who were *tributarii*. Both laws underline their dependence on *dominus*. This then must be the case referred to in the above-mentioned text of Sidonius Apollinaris. All three laws therefore refer to *coloni* and *inquilini* who were, or had become, *adscripticii*. As such, they paid tax through the *dominus* and so were in the position designated by the term *tributarius* which in fact denoted only the fiscal aspect of dependence.[23]

---

23. For *tributarius*, see Segrè, op.cit.; Jones, LRE II 799; Eibach, *Kolonat*, 219ff.

CONCLUSION

1. *Freedom in Danger*

The status of *colonus* as a freeman was not disputed even in the Later Roman Empire. However, his individual rights (to dispose of his property, to change domicile or participate to the public office) were to such a degree limited and subject to the landlord's will, that in one constitution Justinian questions the difference between a *colonus* and a slave when both are in the power of the *dominus*.[1] Although the rhetorical tone of the question cannot be denied, it was rooted in reality. As early as the fifth and sixth centuries, *coloni* are called *servi terrae ipsius cui nati sunt* and are said to be *quadam servitute dediti*. It is true that the difference between *ingenuus colonus* and *servus* remained throughout Roman times; but in legal texts dependent *coloni* are opposed to *coloni* who were *sui iuris ac liberi*, as well as to free peasants, *liberi plebei*.[2]

The question of freedom, in what concerns the social class to which the *coloni* belonged and the time at which the colonate became widespread, arises in its original, fundamental meaning, i.e. as ability to act on one's own free will. Its political aspect, the right to active participation in political life, Roman *libertas* had already been lost at the time the Principate was established. The negative concept of this freedom, *securitas*, namely, protection from abuse of power in the hands of those who were by virtue of their status and position superior to others was no longer of any importance.[3] Individual rights, protected by law on the principle of equality for all—*aequitas iuris*—as the privilege of free Roman citizens, is subsumed in the definition of freedom found in the *Digesta*, IV 3-4: *Summa itaque de iure personarum divisio haec est, quod omnes homines aut liberi sunt aut servi. Libertas est naturalis facultas eius quod cuique facere libet, nisi si quid vi aut iure prohibetur.* This referred to Roman citizens, slavery coming under the heading of *iuris gentium*: *servitus est constitutio iuris gentium qua quis dominio alieno contra naturam subicitur.*[4]

It was this right to act of one's free will that was challenged in

---

1. C.J.XI 48, 21: *Quae etenim differentia inter servos et adscripticios intellegetur cum uterque in domini sui positus est potestate et possit servum cum peculio manumittere et adscripticium cum terra suo dominio expellere?*

2. See *Servi terrae ipsias cui nati sunt* in C.J.XI,52 and *quodam servitute dediti* in C.J.XI 50,2, on the other side *sui iuris ac liberi* in C.J.XI 48, 8.

3. See ch. Foreword.

4. C.J.I 5,4 f.

the case of the *coloni*. But could this have led to a real and complete
loss of freedom?

In considering the legal protection of civil and peregrine *libertas*,
Mommsen emphasizes three points:[5]

1. A Roman citizen could not of his own free will become a non-
citizen or be made unfree. Certain forms of self-alienation, recognized
in earlier laws, were declared invalid in classical Roman law. Getting
into debt was considered, even earlier on, as conditional self-alienation
and unpaid debts led to loss of freedom. These cases also called for
banishment from Roman society. If the indebted party remained in
Roman or Latin communities, the new relationship was regarded as
private enslavement (*privatrechtliche Unfreiheit*);

2. Neither could the Roman citizen become a non-citizen or
unfree by the will of a third person. In the case of being taken
prisoner of war or the disinheriting of a son by his father, exclusion
from the Roman legal sphere would necessarily ensue. Classical
Roman law, however, does not permit this;

3. According to classical law, a Roman citizen could legally lose
his civil rights and liberty through his own fault (imprisonment, *noxae
datio* etc.). Even so, as in the case of indebtedness, loss of freedom was
consequent on expulsion from Roman society.

Mommsen defines ownership or quasi-ownership of a free
person by another as bordering on slavery (*Unfreiheit*). This category
of unfree people played an important part in pre-classical law.
Classical law endeavored to cover both, by ameliorating and limiting
the number of such cases. Self-alienation, which in substance differed
little from debt slavery (*Schuldknechtschaft*) and was recognized in
preclassical Roman law and practiced widely in its early stages, did not
survive in legislation. The ban of debt serfdom was not a privilege
confined only to Rome and Italy; in some countries it existed in pre-
Roman times, in others it spread during the Empire. When personal
rights were concerned, however, self-alienation, despite the principle,
remained in practice. Mommsen mentions cases among the Gaulish
and Germanic tribes, while Mitteis devotes much attention to this
custom in the eastern provinces. [6] Mommsen concludes that there is
no positive proof that free peregrines were allowed to give themselves
as property of a third party within the Roman Empire. To this
conclusion he appends his opinion of the later Roman colonate: *Der
freiwillige Eintritt in den dinglichen Colonat des späteren Rechts, welcher*

---

5. Th. Mommsen, *Bürgerlicher und peregrinischer Freicheitsschutz im römischen Staat*,
Juristische Abhandlungen, Festgabe für Georg Beseler zum 6.Januar
1885,258ff.(Ges.Schr. II,P.1 ff).

6. L. Miteis, *Riechrecht*, 144 ff.

zulässig gewesen zu sein scheint, kann nicht geltend gemacht werden, da deise Stellung die persönliche Freiheit nicht aufhebt.[7] The same principles remain in force in the Later Empire. Although the freedom of a great many *coloni* had been limited, the legal fiction that they were free (*ingenui*) remained, as the whole question of freedom viewed from the standpoint of its fundamental meaning: *ingenuus* is he who is not a slave. From the point of view of individual rights, a *colonus* was to a certain extent, as Augustine puts it, *sub dominio possessorum.*[8] Rent arrears were the primary reason for reducing him to this position. Indebtedness meant that a *colonus* was no longer *sui iuris* in relation to the *dominus fundi,* thus giving the landowner the right to keep him on the estate until the debt had been paid off. This manner of restricting freedom was not a novelty of the Later Roman Empire; working off debts was common practice in the provinces and even in Italy and Rome as early as the age of the Republic.

The position of *colonus* in the Later antiquity, as in previous ages, could not of itself diminish anyone's freedom. This would ensue only when a *colonus* failed to fulfill his obligations. Nor was the colonate of the Later Empire a product of the emperors' fiscal policy. Tax liability, which in the provinces encompassed a far broader section than that formed by *coloni* of the later centuries, could not have created any social stratum or class. Since the landlord was ultimately responsible for paying taxes, he was given the right in the fourth century and subsequently to keep *coloni* on his estate.

The landlord could prevent a *colonus* from leaving the land by his power of *dominus* (*domini potestate*) as well as his patron (*patroni sollicitudine*). This could well have been applied to a client-patron type of relationship and in certain ways, the situation of the *colonus* resembled that of a *cliens.*[9] The Later Roman Empire exploited for fiscal purposes the colonate relationship that evolved in previous centuries; barbarians allowed to settle on Roman territory were also liable for tax.

As explicitly stated in the imperial constitution dating back to the last decade of the fourth century, C.J.XI 52,1 *coloni* were *ingenui.* The essence of their position, designed as *condicio*—the same word is

---

7. Mommsen, op. cit. 14.

8. August. *De civ. Dei* X 1,2: *Non apellantur coloni qui conditionem debent genitali solo propter agriculturam sub dominio possessorum.* Cf. Tab. Albertini XIII,3, ed. Ch. Courtois, L. Leschi, Ch. Perrat, Ch. Saumagne, Paris 1952: *ex culturis suis mancianis sub dominio Fl(avi) Gemini Catullini fl(a)m(inis).*

9. See Sidon. Apoll. *Epist. V* 19. For the time of the Principate, see K.-P. Johne, J. Kuhn, V. Weber, *Die Kolonen in Italien und in den westlichen Provinzen des römischen Reiches,* 1983, 67.

used to designate the position of *curiales*, as well as freemen and slaves[10]—is more closely defined in the laws: *coloni* were *condicioni subditi* (C.J.I 12,9, A.D.466); they were *obnoxii annuis functionibus et debito condicionis* (C.J.XI 50,2, Arcadius and Honorius). While the slaves in *Nov. Valent.* XXXI 6, A.D.451 were *obnoxii condicioni servitutis*, *coloni* were committed by *nexus colonarius*—an expression found in the terminology of debt serfdom. *Nexus adscripticiae condicionis* also appears in C.J.I 3,36, A.D.484 and *vinculum debitae condicionis* in *Nov. Valent.* XXXV from 456 A.D.

Colonus might be fiscally dependent insofar as he existed as a *caput* in the tax-rolls under the name of the land proprietor to whom he was in debt. Thus the *condicio colonaria* could be *adscripticia* and *debita*, as laws in the fourth and fifth century show, for instance *Nov. Valent.* XXXV,3:

> *nullus originarius inquilinus servus vel colonus ad clericale munus accedat neque monachis adgregetur, ut vinculum debitae condicionis evadat*; C.J.XI 50,2: *coloni censibus dumtaxat adscripti sicuti ab his liberi sunt, quibus eos tributa subiectos non faciunt, ita his, quibus annuis functionibus et debito condicionis obnoxii sunt*; C.J.III 38,11 (334 A.D): *agnatio...colonorum adscripticiae condicionis*; C.J.I 3,36 (484 A.D.): *super illos quoque agricolis...qui cum essent adscripticiae nexibus condicionis conscripti.*

It is obvious that the *condicio* of a *colonus* was on the one hand a consequence of his fiscal obligations and on the other of his relation to the landowner. Accordingly, the evolvement of the dependent *colonus* in the Later Empire is viewed in modern historiography either as a result of the fiscal policy promoted by Diocletian and by emperors of the second half of the fourth century, or as the consequence of rent arrears. The legal, papyrological and literary sources analyzed in previous chapters permit the following conclusions:

1. Imperial fiscal policy in the fourth century was not the primary cause of the dependence of *coloni*;

2. this dependence was based on *colonus'* individual relationship with the landlord;

3. acquiring the status of *colonus* was for the most part voluntary. The mere fact of working on another's land did not make a person dependent;

4. in endeavoring to keep agricultural population on the land,

---

10. *Condicio servitutis*: Cic.*Cael*. 75; Caes. BG III 10,3; *condicio libertatis*: Caes. BG I 28,5. For other examples, see Th.LL s.v. *Condicio*.

even those who did not own it, the Later Roman state gave the right to *domini fundi* to prevent *coloni* from leaving their estate;

5. the purpose of the state was not to protect the interests of the landowning aristocracy. In some legal texts from the fifth and sixth centuries emperors strove to limit the dependence of *coloni* on landowners.

The Roman fiscal system (which did not include Italy until the reign of Diocletian), from its inception could function only under condition that those who worked the land remain on it permanently. Ultimately, it was the landowner who was liable for tax payment. But the tax obligation could be taken over by a tenant by virtue of a contract between him and the landlord. In the early centuries of the Empire, as in the time of the Later Republic, the Roman government did not concern itself with the way in which a landowner would retain a *colonus* who had not fulfilled his obligations, including the paying of taxes. Several documents from Egypt—and there is no reason to believe that it was different in the other provinces—indicate that at the time of a *census* everyone was to register at his place of birth, that is, where he had been entered in the tax-rolls. It was the duty of the provincial governor to return those who had fled from the land for purpose of tax evasion. To prevent the flight, the emperors in the last centuries of the Roman Empire enacted a penalty for those who sheltered fugitives. The first known edict that prescribes a penalty for taking in someone else's ὑπόφορος (*tributarius*), as a man indebted to another and obliged to pay taxes, dates from the time of the Severan dynasty. By protecting the landlord whose *tributarius* had absconded, the government was in fact protecting its own fiscal interests. Although the document is preserved on an Egyptian papyrus, that the fine is stated in sesterces bears witness to its universal application.[11] The policy which, in preventing *coloni iuris alieni* from leaving the land, in fact protected fiscal interests, was carried out as early as Constantine, as the law of 332 A.D., C.Th. V 17 1 testifies. Subsequently it was put into effect by emperors in the second half of the fourth century, in the constitutions of Valentinianus, Valens, Gratianus and Theodosius who, in the law on Palaestinian *coloni* authorizing landowners to retain their *coloni*, calls upon *lex a maioribus constituta.*[12]

These constitutions are the direct consequence of legal regulations dating from the seventh decade of the fourth century and pertaining to land possessors' tax liability: whoever owned land paid

11. D. Thomas, JEA 61. 1975, 219.

12. C.J.XI 51,1.

his own taxes; a *colonus* had to pay tax through the landowner or his agents. A *colonus* could only be taxed together with the land he cultivated and a proprietor was liable for tax on land he owned only if he had laborers on it. On the large estates *coloni* were the main workforce. As far as the fiscal authorities were concerned, only those who possessed land existed as a name. Those working the land not belonging to them were an anonymous number included in the total of *capita*. The latter were, however, the element without which the complex tax system *capitatio-iugatio* could not have functioned. As the law on Thracian *coloni* shows, not even the *iugatio* could be paid if a *colonus*, released from *capitatio* left the land. It was for this reason that landlords were given the right to keep *coloni* by force, as *domini terrae*.[13] This was the most significant innovation of the Later Empire in this field. It was obviously not a case of a privilege bestowed on the influential aristocracy, as is sometimes thought,[14] but primarily a measure to protect the fiscal interests of the state.

Constitutions enshrining the rights accorded to a *dominus terrae* could rely on the private, legal relationship between him and a *colonus* who had fallen behind with his rent and could not leave the estate until he had worked off his debt. Laws, as early as Constantine's law of 332 A.D., C.Th.V 17,1, were concerned with *coloni iuris alieni*. The same category is referred to in laws on *coloni* from Thrace, Illyricum and Palestine. The emperor could in such cases quite properly call upon *mos maiorum* and the right of the *dominus* to demand that debts be worked off. The indebted *coloni* spoken of by Pliny,[15] who on account of rent arrears had lost their *peculium* and any hope of repaying their debts, had they lived after Diocletian when Italy had become a part of the general fiscal system, would have also lost the right to leave the land they lived on.

There remain two cases of restricting a *colonus'* right to leave the

---

13. C.Th. V 17,1; C.J. XI 52,1 and others.

14. See Jones, *Colonate*, 300; A.V.Koptev, in his paper about "freedom" of *coloni*, VDI 1990/2, 37 concludes that the civil rights of the *coloni* and their status as free people were in danger because the landlords gained power over them not only as consequence of the contract, but as a politically influential class. Koptev, one of the few modern authors to discuss personal freedom of the Later Roman *coloni*, tries to trace the process of diminishing freedom of once free tenants from the early fourth century, when, he thinks, the *coloni* were first prohibited from leaving their place of origin, to the fifth century, when they were treated as semidependent and close to slaves. The turning point in this process would be from the last decades of the fourth to the first decades of fifth century. See also his paper in VDI 1989/4,33ff.

15. For instance Pliny. *Epist.III* and the commentary of A.N. Sherwin-White, *The Letters of Pliny, A Historical and Sociological Commentary*, 1966,256 ff; *Epist.* IX 37,2. Cf. D.Kehoe, *Chiron* 18,1988, 38ff.; P.Brunt, JRS 52(1962): 71, n.31.

land that are hard to justify: first, the hereditary aspect of the *colonus'* status and second, the binding of those classed as free *coloni* to the land that they cultivated for more than thirty years. Both cases, however, do lean on prior practice. The descendants of *coloni* in the fifth and sixth centuries could not leave the land that "their fathers had taken upon themselves to work."[16] Among them undoubtedly were those whose fathers' *reliqua* prevented them from leaving the estate and possibly whose fathers while still living had taken upon themselves to work off their debts and rent arrears. The hereditary character of this kind of debt could be defended from the legal aspect by analogy with earlier practice, mentioned in the *Digesta*, whereby the descendant of a *colonus* would even when he himself was not a *colonus*, assume his father's obligations in the case of his death.[17] This practice in time apparently became widespread. Accordingly, all laws related to fugitives demand the restoration of *coloni* together with their descendants.[18] The *condicio colonaria* was passed on from one generation to the next. When fourth generation *coloni* revolted on Libanius' estate, he accused them of "not wanting to remain what they were." The penalty with which they were threatened was a prison sentence.[19]

Among those who inherited the status of *colonus* were also those whose fathers had not been *coloni iuris alieni*, but *liberi coloni* who disposed of their own *peculium* and were *sui arbitri* and could therefore upon the expiration of their lease go to another landowner. Anastasius' law was the first to deprive a free *colonus* of the right to abandon the land once he had worked on it for more than thirty years, CJ.XI,48,23:

---

16. C.J.XI 48,23.

17. Dig. XIX 2,60,1: *Heredem coloni, quamvis colonus non est, nihilo minus domino possidere existimo.*

18. C.J.XI 52,1 (cum omni peculio et agnatione); cf. also C.J.XI 48, 23. Giving up children to work off debts was a widespread practice, cf. e.g. P. Flor. 44 (A.D. 158), P. Tebt. 384 (A.D. 10), P. Mich 121 (third century) and others. Diocletian tried to prevent this by law (C.J. VIII 16,6, from A.D. 293 or C.J. IV 10,12 A.D. 294). A case of this kind is discussed in letters of St. Augustine, see M. Humbert, *Enfants à louer et à vendre, Augustin et l'authorité parentalle (Epist. 10* et 24*)*, Les lettres de saint Augustin, découvertes par Johannes Divjak, Communications présentés au Colloque 1982, 189ff.; see also M. Meyer, *Pfandvertrag zwecks Auslösung einer durch den Vater verpfändeten Tochter, Juristische Papyri*, (1902), 29 f.

19. Lib.*Or.* XLVII 13: Ἰουδαῖοι τῶν πανὺ, γῆν ἡμῖν πολὺν ἐργαζόμενοι χρόνον γενεὰς τέτταρας ἐπεθύμησαν μὴ ὅπερ ἦσαν εἶναι καὶ τὸν παλαιόν ἀποσεισάμενοι ζυγὸν ἠξίουν ὁρισταὶ τοῦ πῶς ἡμῖν αὐτοῖς χρηστέον εἶναι. See L. Harmand, *Discours sur les patronages* (1955), 135ff.

Τῶν γεωργῶν οἱ μὲν ἐναπόγραφοι οἱ εἰσιν καὶ τὰ τούτων πεκούλια τοῖς δεσπόταις ἀνήκει, οἱ δὲ χρόνῳ τῆς τριακονταετίας μισθωτοὶ γίνονται ἐλεύθεροι μένοντες μετὰ τῶν πραγμάτων αὐτῶν. καὶ οὗτοι δὲ ἀναγκάζονται καὶ τὴν γῆν γεωργεῖν καὶ τὸ τέλος παρέχειν. τοῦτο δὲ καὶ τῷ δεσπότῃ καὶ τοῖς γεωργοῖς λυσιτελές.

Justinian extended this to include the descendants of free *coloni*, albeit recognizing their right to remain free and dispose of their *peculium*.[20]

When assessing the importance of these imperial constitutions, two factors should be taken into consideration: one, that the landowner's right to reclaim a *colonus* within thirty years was recognized in some cases even before 419 A.D.[21] and second, that these decrees initially referred only to dependent *coloni*, those who were *originarii* (C.Th.V 18,1) and *obnoxii* (*Nov.Valent.* XXXI). The law in Theodosian Code, dating back to the year 400 A.D., C.Th. XII 19, 2, also refers to a thirty- or forty-years period:

As public interests should come before private ones, it is decreed that whosoever spends thirty consecutive years within the province or forty consecutive years outside the province serving the curia, collegium or in a stronghold, cannot be reclaimed on account of colonatus or inquilinatus, be it a case of imperial or private land.[22]

Novella Valentiniani XXXI strives to prevent abuse of this law, as *coloni* succeeded in absconding by frequently changing estates and landowners. The emperor tried to deter those who "would gain by flight the freedom they did not have by birth."[23]

---

20. C.J.XI 48, 23.

21. C.Th.V 18,1, A.D. 418: *Si quis colonus originalis vel inquilinus ante hos triginta annos de possessione discessit neque ad solum genitale silentii continuatione repetitus est, omnis ab ispo vel a quo forte possidetur calumnia penitus excludatur quem annorum numerum futuris quoque temporibus volumus observari*; cf. also Nov. Va.. XXXI.—These and the legal texts quoted in the following notes show clearly that the regulation of the longi temporis praescriptio could be applied to the coloni, E. Chiusi, Dr. Titiana München in a Letter). That means the *coloni* were treated as a property of the *dominus terrae*.

22. C.Th.XII 19,2: *Eum igitur qui curiae vel collegio vel burgis ceterisque corporibus intra eandem provinciam per XXX annos in alia XL sine interpellatione servierit, neque res dominica neque actio privata continget, si colonatus quis aut inquilinatus quaestionem movere temptaverit.*

23. See Nov. Val. XXXI,1: *Ita contigit, ut, cum illi pereat a quo fugit nec huic ad quem venit possit adquiri, mansionum permutatione desinat esse quod natus est, libertatem*

From the texts quoted above, it is clear that no one had the right to reclaim a *colonus* who had spent thirty consecutive years outside the estate, regardless of whether he was by origin *colonus iuris alieni* or *originarius*. In either case if the *colonus* stayed on the land where he had worked for thirty years, he became bound to it. The Emperor Anastasius applied this principle to *coloni* who were free to dispose of themselves and their *peculium*, deeming it beneficial to both landlord and *colonus*: it was beneficial to the landowner as he retained laborers on the land, with the possibility of keeping their descendants as well; a *colonus* on the other hand, gained the right to remain on the land he had cultivated, and could not be evicted in old age. He stayed there for his lifetime. Ultimately, it was the government that profited most: by keeping free *coloni* on the land, it ensured the payment of taxes. Consequently the liberty of free *coloni* was restricted. This constitution for fiscal purposes equals the position of *coloni* who did not own land with those who did: neither could leave the land on which he was enrolled in the tax-lists as *caput*, the land on which taxes had been levied.

Justinian's prescription that the children of free *coloni* must also stay on the land their fathers worked had no legal justification, although they were guaranteed their freedom and the right to dispose of their *peculium*.[24] It merely resolved the problem of how to bind to the land those who did not own it. Proclaiming them free was official hypocrisy and empty words. One of Arcadius' and Honorius' constitutions, sent to Nebridius, the *comes* of Asia, C.J.XI 50,2, rests on the statement that *coloni* are committed to some kind of a slavery, regardless of whether they are *censibus asdcripti* or relieved of it. They are subjugated to those to whom they owe both by annual payments and debts, *annuis functionibus et debito condicionis*. After the late fifth and early sixth centuries, law restricted the real freedom of free *coloni*; Justinian extended this regulation on descendants of those who spent more than thirty years on the same estate, thus reducing the children of free *coloni* to the status of *originarii*.

2. *Escape from Freedom*

Despite all this, no one freeman was actually forced into becoming a *colonus*. Both in the Later Roman Empire and during the earlier centuries, people entered voluntarily and willingly into this

---

quam nascendo non habuit, fugae sibi adsiduitate defendens. Cf. similar in Lib. *Or. XLVII,13, cit.* in n. 19.

24. C.J. XI 48 19 and XI 48, 23.

type of relationship. Working on someone else's land as a *colonus* did not necessarily lead to loss of freedom. [25] Neither did anyone become a dependent *colonus* merely because fiscal liability prevented him from leaving the land. It was not rare, however, for penury to drive those who had no property (and therefore no guarantee that they could fulfill their obligations to the landowner) when appealing to a landlord to take them on, to accept in advance all kinds of conditions, even those that would obviously lead to a loss of their freedom. Numerous documents on ἐναπόγραφοι in Egypt testify to this. Appealing to the landlord to take him on his land, the ἐναπόγραφος mortgages all he possesses, including his family and himself, similar to those in the *paramoné* documents, and obliges himself to do all that the landowner shall require of him. In some cases others vouch for him, taking upon themselves the obligation of endeavoring to return the ἐναπόγραφος in the case of his flight. Should they fail in this, they guarantee that they themselves will work in his stead.

The burden of fiscal liability may have made a certain number of free peasants seek refuge as *coloni* on wealthy estates. Many of these in Gaul, fleeing the tax agents, abandoned their farms and with them, their freedom. As Salvianus in *De gub. dei V* 39ff. testifies, the former free peasants *et rerum proprietate careant et ius libertatis amittant*— "and in losing their land, they lose the liberty," and were deprived not only of their property but also of their status—*extores non facultatis tantum sed etiam condicionis*, for they subject themselves to the conditions of the *inquilinus, iugo se inquilinae abiectionis addicunt.* As they no longer possessed their land, they did not pay tax in their own name; they were included in the number of *capita* on the estate of the person whose land they had to cultivate in the future.

Many groups of barbarians, defeated in war or by their own will were permitted to live in the Roman state. Those who by requesting permission from the Roman emperors to settle on Roman territory, cultivated the land as dependent *coloni*, paid taxes and were subject to Roman law, renouncing their freedom voluntarily. Belonging to the social class of *coloni* improved the position of those who entered the Roman state as prisoners of war, later to be distributed to landowners to cultivate the land as *tributarii* or *coloni*. Their position is to be compared to that of slaves who became *coloni*, *servi quasi coloni*. In the imperial constitution dating from the early fifth century, the barbarian Scyri are given guarantees that they will

---

25. As it could not change his juristic status, in the Later Empire as well as in the Principate, for the latter, see Nörr, "Zur sozialen und rechtlichen Bewertung der freien Arbeit in Rom," *ZSS* 82, (1965): 86 ff.

not be used in any way except as *coloni adscripticii*.[26]   Possessing
neither property nor freedom when they entered the estate, they had
to be treated as *coloni iuris alieni*.

It is apparent that the reasons for people entering the colonate,
with the concomitant restrictions of their freedom, were various. Frequently it was a case of a flight from freedom, one that could not
provide security and had therefore become an intolerable burden, as
Erich Fromm puts it.[27] It was from freedom of this kind that men fled
into subjugation.

3. *Libertas recuperata*

The Constitution of Arcadius and Honorius, C.J.XI 50,2, states
at the outset that *coloni*, whether liable for or exempt from taxes, are
rather like slaves of a kind: *Coloni censibus dumtaxat adscripti, sicuti ab
his liberi sunt, quibus eos tributa subiectos non faciunt, ita his, quibus
annuis functionibus et debito condicionis obnoxii sunt, paene est ut
quadam servitute dediti videantur.* The question naturally arises
whether there was a possibility for those who had become *coloni iuris
alieni* and dependent upon the landlords, as well as those who, because
of taxation, had been forced into permanent tenancy on another's
land to recover their freedom to leave the land if they so desired and
go wherever they wished.

This question might be considered from various aspects: First,
could the *colonus* set himself free from the *condicio colonaria?* Second,
could the landlord of his own free will, in view of the fact that private
debts were the primary reason for restricting the freedom of the
colonus, release him from his obligation and thereby from his status
of *colonus?* Finally, did the Roman state ever release anyone from his
obligations as a *colonus*, or when indebtedness of *coloni* had become
a widespread occurrence, did it take any measures to prevent or
ameliorate their position, as the Athenian state had done with
indebted peasants in the early sixth and the Egyptian state in the
eighth century B.C.?

* * *

1. The *colonus* was undoubtedly able to acquire the right to
depart from the land he cultivated on the condition that he fulfilled
his obligations towards the proprietor, or acquired land of his own
which would be sufficient to support him. This, however, was
apparently very rare. Indebted *coloni* even in the time of Pliny,

---

26. C.Th. V 6, 3.

27. E. Fromm, *Escape from Freedom,* 38.

discouraged by an accumulation of rent arrears, were no longer trying to reduce it. In the Later Roman Empire the rent arrears of *colonus* became a widespread phenomenon. Evidence of people freeing themselves from such a position by their own labor is also rare. One example might be an inscription from Maktar in Bizacena, CIL VIII 11824 (ILS 7457; CLE 1238). It seems to have been an *originarius* in question, born on land probably cultivated by his parents, poor and without *census*: *paupere progenitus lare sum parvoq. parente cuius non census neque domus fuerat.* He himself cultivated the land on which he was born: *ex quo sum genitus, ruri mea vixi colendo.* By his own labors, he succeeded in redeeming himself from the position into which he had been born. At first he was a reaper, then a *ductor,* until finally, after eleven years of work, he had his own house and *villa*; he became a *curialis* and then a *censor.* No legal obstacle blocked his transition from one class to the other. It was thus possible for dependent *coloni* and *inquilini* to free themselves from their status, but one can hardly believe that it happened frequently.

Judging from the legal texts, the dependent *coloni* mainly attempted to free themselves from a position of dependence and debt by flight that usually ended on the estate of another landlord. Some sought escape in holy orders or tried to become *curiales*, while the law strove to prevent both. Even attempted escape called down harsh reprisals. With the introduction of a limitation of the possibility of leaving an estate after a work thirty years long (*longi temporis praescriptio*), the *coloni* endeavored to avoid this by frequent changes of domicile and landowner, thereby "acquiring freedom they did not have by birth." Imperial constitutions made every effort to prevent this as well.[28]

2. Landlords of the Later Empire were accorded far-reaching authority over dependent, indebted *coloni*. The state intervened only when its fiscal interests were threatened. In all other aspects the colonate system was treated—as it had been in the time of the Principate—as a private arrangement between *colonus* and *dominus fundi.*[29] The conclusion to be drawn is that the Roman state did not

---

28. The Later Roman state was reluctant to erase from the tax-rolls *capita* once they had been inscribed, even when this was necessary, as in the case of a peasant's death. Eusebius, *Vita const.* I6, criticizes Emperor Licinius for keeping on the tax-lists those who died in order to demand tax from the landowner whose land they had cultivated. Procopius in his *Hist.-arc.XI* 29 f. speaks similarly of Justinian: he levied taxes from a proprietor whose land was cultivated by Samartians, in the meantime killed in the war.

29. Juristic status of *colonus* was of no importance for the landlord. In a letter, *Ad Salvium*, Sulpicius Severus for instance has no idea of the legal position of the people working in his fields and calls them *rusticuli mei, homines mei, coloni,* cf. C. Lepelly,

interfere in a landowner's choosing to release a *colonus* from part of his payment or write off his debts—a conclusion which is borne out by various ancient authors. From Libanius, Or.XLVII c.20ff., it may be inferred that he considers it natural that the fate of his *coloni* should depend on him as *dominus*. That the landlord could release the *colonus* from his position and allow him to become a *liber plebeius*, one who worked on his own land for which he paid tax, is evident from a letter of Sidonius Apollinaris, Ep. V 19: in a dispute with a neighbor proprietor whose *colonus* had seduced his *ancilla*, Sidonius suggests that the former should be released from his position of *originalis inquilinatus*, thus becoming a free person or *plebeius*: *mox cliens factus e tributario plebeiam potius incipiat habere personam quam colonariam.* This, by all appearances, did not mean that the ex-*colonus* could abandon the land he had cultivated and on which as a freeman he had to pay tax.

   3. It is often thought that the Roman state in the last centuries of its existence assisted in a process which led to restriction on the freedom of the *colonus*, tying him to the *dominus terrae*, thus ensuring regular payment of taxes. There is no doubt that the Roman state had always tried to prevent the rural population in the provinces from leaving the land and that it protected its fiscal interests. In the Later Empire, when indebtedness had become a widespread phenomenon, the state could intervene in several ways: by writing off debts, whether fiscal or private, or by prohibiting restrictions of freedom because of debt, as it had done in the past. It could assist smallholders to hold on to their land or *coloni* to achieve it. It could, ultimately, have found a new method of relieving the position of the indebted, but the Later Roman state did not follow any of these possibilities. The only documented way was by a partial abolition of the tax.

   The abolition of the *capitatio*, a tax which depended on the number of people who paid it, took place at the end of the fourth century in the provinces in Thrace and Illyricum that had been hardest hit by the oliganthropy. This measure did not reduce the burden on owners of land while not releasing anyone from *iugatio terrena*. As those who had no land were tied to the land by private debts to the landlord, imperial law neither abolished debts neither ameliorated their position. Between two goals, to ameliorate the position of the people cultivating the land or to secure the taxes, the Roman state preferred the latter.

   There is, however, evidence that the Later Empire legislation attempted in some cases to slow down the disappearance due to the

---

Antiquites africaines 25, (1989): 235ff. Similar was with Palladius, cf. Ed. Frezouls, "La vie rurale aux Bas-Empire d'apres l'oeuvre de Palladius," *Ktema* 5 (1980): 193ff.

debt of peasant freeholders: in several *Novellae* Justinian warns the governors of the Danubian provinces not to allow creditors to constrain the land (*terrulas*) of poverty-stricken peasants unable to pay back interest of loans of tiny quantities of wheat. Debt and interest repayment were also regulated by law.[30]

The most efficacious way of keeping the landless on the farms they cultivated—and in the same time reducing the number of wandering beggers—was to enable the landlords to prevent them as private debtors from leaving. This was a new departure for the Later Roman Empire: although released from the *capitatio, coloni* in the most cases were unable to leave because of their private debts and obligations to the landowners. By remaining to cultivate the land, they facilitated the payment of the *iugatio*.

Finally, the question of descendants remains. Whether these were dependent or free, were they obliged to remain on the land their parents cultivated more than thirty years? Were they able to attain their freedom and leave the farm on which they were born and raised? Justinian's *Novella* 162,2 allows such a possibility, on condition that they obtain land of their own, sufficient to support them and their families. By achieving land capable of doing so, even the descendant of *adscripticius* ceased to be a *colonus* and became a *possessor* registered in the tax-rolls under his own name, together with his farm. He was no longer *censibus adscriptus*, but an *inscriptus*, as formulated in Justinian's *Novella* 128,14, *inscriptus propriam habere possessione*. Even then he had to remain on the land, not as a *colonus* but as a free peasant registered together with his land in the tax-rolls under his own name.

* * *

Later Roman legislations reveals the difference between two basic groups which formed the free rural population in the Empire: one were freeholders, among whom were large landowners, but also the *plebei*; the other were *coloni.* The factor that united the first in a group is that both the proprietor of the large estates and small freeholders, *plebei*, possessed land registered in the tax-rolls under their own names, together with the number of *capita* working on it. A key feature of the latter group was that they did not have their own

---

30. Nov.Just. XXXIV:*Venit enim   ad nostras aures quosdam in Mysia Secunda provincia quam administras avare temporum necessitate captata ad quosdam feneraticias fecisse contractus et paucam mensuram fructuum dantes totas terrulas eorum abstraxisse et ex hac causa quosdam colonorum fugae latebras petisse, alios fame esse necatos et tristissimam pestem homines invasisse incursione barbarica non minorem...See further: Nemini penitus eorum audente terrulas detineri sub occasione feneraticiae cautionis sive in sine scripti credita sunt contracta.*

land or not have sufficient to earn a livelihood for themselves and their families, but worked as tenant on another's land. This difference was inherited from previous centuries. At the time of the Later Empire, the number of those working as *coloni* was numerous and, for various reasons, increased with time. Many small holders lost their possessions because of debt; debt was hereditary and therefore had to be worked off by their descendants; the tax burden forced some of the free peasants to leave their land possession and to work as *coloni*; the number in this group was also increased by settling barbarians who were granted the status of *coloni*.

There are several terms designating those who worked another's land: *adscripticii* (*enapographoi*), *inquilini*, *originarii*, *tributarii* (*hypophoroi*). Modern research explains their occurrence in various ways. It is clear that some of the terms, such as *adscripticius* or *tributarius*, mainly indicate position in relation to taxation. This is nonetheless a consequence of their real position in relation to the landlord. *Coloni* differed in degree of economic dependence and were actually divided into two groups: 1. *Coloni iuris alieni* and 2. *Liberi coloni*, who were *sui arbitri*.

This division is clearly formulated from the legal point of view in the law of Emperor Anastasius: on one hand there were *adscripticii* whose *peculium* was at the disposal of the landlord; on the other were free *coloni* (*liberi*) who had their own property, cultivated the land which does not belong to them and paid tax. Penalties in the case of actual flight from the land or even planning escape, were envisaged only in the case of *colonus iuris alieni*; those who sheltered them would also be obliged to pay tax due for the period which had elapsed. *Liberi coloni* were, if they fled, treated similarly to *liberi plebei*. As they paid their own taxes, they were simply returned to the land without being subjected to any penalties.

The freedom of a *colonus* who was *iuris alieni* was bounded by *ius* and indebted they were treated as *addicti* or *iudicati*. Their debts tied them to one landowner and one estate. Restriction of the freedom of dependent *colonus* was reflected in the fact that he could no longer dispose of his *peculium* because he had mortgaged it. As he had no property, he did not pay taxes independently in his own name, but was registered on the tax-rolls under the name of the proprietor. He could not sell his *peculium* without the approval of the landlord, nor could he bequeath his property even to the church. He could not appear as a witness in court against the *dominus fundi*; he was not allowed to take *creationes*, i.e. public office in urban administration without the approval of the landlord; without his permission the *colonus* could not take holy orders either.

Some of these restrictions existed in earlier practice. The condition that all that *colonus* brought with him on the estate where he worked would serve as pledge (*pignus*) might lead to the landlord's selling it in order to recover his claim from the *colonus*. As *pignus* could serve crops from the field, so that the *colonus* could not lay claim to them until he had paid back what he owed to the landlord. *Reliqua colonorum* were included in legacies and patrimony and had to be taken into account, along with the lease and the *coloni* themselves, in the case of the sale of land or the death of the proprietor. Thus was created the bond tying the *colonus* to the land and which could disappear only when he had fulfilled his obligations. The question of taxation was settled often with an agreement between landowner and *colonus* and there were cases, even before Diocletian where the *colonus* was entered on the tax-roll under the name of the landlord.[31]

None of the restrictions of the freedom of the *colonus* can be linked to the time of Diocletian; neither can the regulation that a person giving shelter to another's *tributarius* was fiscally liable. This throws doubt on the idea, widely held in modern historiography, that Diocletian's fiscal reform brought about the dependence of the *coloni*. The Roman state directly influenced the status of the *coloni* by authorizing the landlord to retain on his land those who had been entered for tax purposes as *coloni* in the total number of *capita*. The Roman authorities were chiefly interested in the person who was *adscriptus censibus* and whom it could not retain on the land because it did not belong to him. Hence *adscripticius* is the most frequent term used in Later Roman legislation on the *coloni*.

The *coloni* themselves were aware of the difference between freedom and dependence, even when paying taxes through an intermediary. In the papyrological text from the fifth century, P.Ross. Geogr. III 8, the γεωργοί warn the δεσπότης that, although they pay taxes through him, they are not his slaves, just as they were not slaves of his father of grandfather:

Γινόσκιν σε θελώμεν, κύριε ἡμῶν Νέχαι, ὅτι οὐδαι ἐπὶ
τοῦ πάτρος σοῦ οὐδε ἐπεὶ τῆς εὐπυίας σοῦ τὸ σόμα
δεδωκάμεν ἀλλὰ. ὃς ἡνιαύσιος ποιοῦμεν τὸ ἐ [ν]τάγιον
παρέχομεν οὐδένι.

In contrast to this, ἐναπόγραφοι in some other documents are

---

31. For this category, see L. Varcl, Μετρηματιαιοι, *JJP* 11/12,(1958):97ff.; D. Rathbone, *Economic Rationalism and Rural Society in Third-Century Egypt*, (1992), 116ff. .

reconciled in advance to the idea of serving the landlord and call themselves ὑμέτεροι δοῦλοι and are ready to undertake to do all that δεσπότης, i.e. the landowner shall require of them. This reflects the difference between free *coloni* or *adscripticii* and dependent, those who lost their freedom.

APPENDIX

As basis for translation of laws collected in *Codex Theodosianus* is used C. Pharr, *The Theodosian Code and Novels and the Sirmondian Constitutions, a translation with commentary, glossary and bibliography*, New York, 1952.

C.Th. V 17,1
Date: 332 A.D.
Emperor Constantine Augustus to the Provincials.

Any person with whom the *colonus* that belongs to another is found not only shall restore him to the place of his origin,* but also to assume the capitation tax for the time elapsed. It is also allowed to bound in chain the *coloni* who meditate flight in the same manner as they were slaves, so that they shall be forced to fulfil their duties that befit freemen by virtue of the slave's sentence.

Interpretation: If any person should knowingly detain in his own household a *colonus* that belongs to another, he shall first restore the man himself to his owner and he shall be compelled to pay his tribute for as long a time as the man was with him. But the *colonus* himself who was unwilling to be what he had been born shall be reduced to slavery.

C.Th. XI 1, 14 (C.J. XI 48,4)
Date: 336 A.D. (372 vel 374? Mai 1)

If any person have the ownership of the great estates (*fundorum dominia*)** he shall accept the responsibility either through himself or his own overseers*** for tax collection **** and shall assume the fulfillment of the duties of this compulsory service for those *coloni* who were born to their condition and who are proved to have been enrolled on the tax lists on such lands.

Of course, We exclude from any part of this regulation those persons who have possession of any small plot of land if they are enrolled on their own plots of land under their own name in the tax lists, for they must be assigned to their mediocre status and they must assume the payments of taxes in kind under the direction of the customary tax collectors.

*to his birth status, Pharr
**Of any field, Pharr
***for compulsion, Pharr
**** Pharr links the words *through himself or his overseer* with the *ownership of the land* in the precedent sentence.

C.J.XI 53,1
Date: 371 A.D.

We declare that the *coloni* and *inquilini* in Illyricum and neighboring regions cannot have permission to depart from the fields in which it is certain that they dwell by virtue of birth and paternity. They have to be attached to the land not by virtue of their tax obligation but by their name and title *coloni*, so that if they depart or pass over to another (*dominus?*) they are to be recalled and subjected to penalties and chains. For those who calculate that an alien and unknown person is to be received would remain a penalty, both in compensation of the working days and in damage that was done to the places that were deserted, as well as a fine whose amount we leave to the determination of the judge. Even the landlord of the possession in which the *alienus* (*colonus*) is shown is to be forced to undergo punishment to the extent of the quality of his mistake. The ignorance is no excuse because only the fact that he kept a person unknown to him suffices to determine that crime has taken place.

Cf. slightly different translation by Goffart, *Caput and Colonate*, p.80.

C.Th.X 12,2-4
Date: 368? 370? 373?
Emperors Valentinian and Valens to Probus the Preatorian Prefect
2. If any *tributarius* * should be found or an *inquilinus* indicated, he shall return immediately to that person to whose ownership he declares that he is subject.
3. Nevertheless, the investigation shall proceed to the point that searching out everything the governor shall learn whether the instigator of the petition was a person who was under the necessity to gloss over with some pretext the outrage of an unjust retention. Thus if any person should seek by such contrivance to harbor *coloni*, he shall make good the loss of tribute. If he should seek to harbor slaves, he shall be held to that punishment which was formerly established by law.
4. Moreover, if any person should assert that he is a plebeian or free (*colonus*) **, after he was proved the trustworthiness of his claim, he shall be vindicated from all annoyance and shall be returned to that locality from which he becomes evident that he came.

* *If any person should be found to be subject to tribute or should be an inquilinus*, Pharr,
** Free man, Pharr, in the Latin text only *liber*.

C.J.XI 48,8
Date:370s

Emperors Valentinianus an Valens Augusteses to Probus the Praetorian Prefect.

All fugitives who had placed themselves under somebody's protection shall be recalled together with the tax obligation using all moderation in this, so if the person with whom they are found should know that they belong to another man and if he should use the fugitive to his own profit, i.e. so that they should cultivate land that brings fruits to the owner and the owner should allow to the fugitive to retain a part of the harvest for himself but without receiving the reward due for this work, the owner of the estate shall be liable for the tax what the state finances had lost. But if the fugitive should conceal that they belong to another man and should place themselves on somebody's land as *sui arbitri* and should cultivate the land either giving a part of the fruits due to the owner for the land and keeping the rest for themselves as their *peculium* or receiving any sort of reward for their work, the fugitive shall pay the taxes due because it is clear that the private contract is in the question. If among the farmers, as it happens, should be found a debtor of any kind or in any business, the judge shall made request of what is due after he constitutes the parties publicly.

C.J.XI 51,1
Date: 393s

Emperors Valentinianus, Theodosius et Arcadius Augusteses to Cynegio the Praetorian Prefect.

As a law established by our ancestors, detaining *coloni* by eternal right, so that they are not allowed to depart from those places from whose they collect harvest or desert those fields that they once undertook to cultivate, in force in all other provinces, do not support the landlords in the province of Palaestina, we decree that in Palaestina too no *colonus* may rejoice in independence as if he were a person *sui iuris* free and vagrant and would go, but as in the other provinces he is to be held to the landlord so that he could not depart without punishment upon one who receive him. To this is added that all authority to recall him is granted to the landlord.

C.J.XI 52,1
Date: 396s

Throughout the dioceses of Thrace the register of the *capitation* tax liability is canceled forever and only land tax is to be paid. In order to prevent that the *coloni* absolved from paying of the tax obligation appear to have allowed to wander and to depart whatever they wish, let them be held by right of origin. Although they appear to be free in status, they have to be treated as slaves of the land to which they were born and let them have no possibility to withdraw when they wish or go on another place, but landlord should use the right either as *patronus* with solitude or as a master with his power.

If any person believes that he could receive or retain a colonus belong to another man, he shall be forced to pay two pounds gold to the man whose fields *colonus* deprived of cultivation by his flight and to restore him with all his property and his progenies.

C.Th.V 6,3
Date: 409 A.D.

Emperors Honorius and Theodosius to Anthemius, Praetorian Prefect.

We have subjected the Scyrae, a barbarian tribe, to Our power after We had routed a very great force of Chuni, their ally. Therefore We grant to all persons the opportunity to supply their own fields with men of the aforesaid people. But all persons shall know that they shall hold those whom they have received by no other title than that of *colonus* and that no one shall be permitted either fraudulently to take anyone of those *coloni* away from the person to whom he had once been assigned or to receive such a one as a fugitive, under the penalty which is inflicted upon those who harbor persons that are registered in the tax-rolls of others or *coloni* who do not belong to them.

1. Moreover, the owners of lands may use the free labor of such captives, but no one shall be forced to undergo a tax equalization for the tax-rolls...; and no one shall be permitted to transfer such persons, as though they had to be given to him, from the obligations of the tax declaration to that of slavery or use them for urban duties. Those who receive such persons shall be permitted, because of the shortage of farm produce, to retain them for a two-year period in any provinces they please, provided that these provinces are across the sea and thereafter to place them in permanent homes, their residence in the regions of Thrace and Illyricum shall be absolutely prohibited to them, but within a five-year period shall it be permitted to make a transfer openly and freely within the confines of the same province. The furnishing of recruits also shall be suspended during the aforesaid twenty-year period. The distribution of these people throughout the transmarine provinces shall be made to those who so wish through petitions to apply to your court.

C.Th.XI 24,6,1-4
Date: 415 A.D.

Emperors Honorius and Theodosius Augusteses to Aurelianus Augustalianus Preatorian Prefect.

The examination of Valerius, Theodosius and Tharsacius shall cease and in the court of the augustal prefect only those persons shall be prosecuted who from the time of the consulship of Caesarius and Atticus have begun to possess landholdings under the title of patrocinium.* However, We decree that all such persons shall be subject to the payment of state taxes,** so that the name of patron shall be judged to be completely abolished. Moreover, the landholdings that are still established in their own status shall remain under the control of the former landholders, if in accordance with the antiquity of the tax lists they will undoubtedly assume their proportionate share in the taxes payment and liturgies*** which the *homologi coloni* are known to provide.

1. But the *metrocomiae* shall continue under the public law which shall remain unchanged, not shall any person attempt possession of such villages or any property in them, unless he has undoubtedly begun such possessions before the aforesaid consulship; but the fellow villagers shall be excepted to whom they cannot deny the payment that must be made in accordance with the condition of their fortune.

2. If any person, contrary to custom, should obtain possession of small fertile landholdings in the villages themselves, according the proportion of his holding he may not refuse the unproductive land and its tax and compulsory public services.

3. Of course, if any persons called in the native manner *homologi*, shoud desert the villages to which they are assigned and should pass either to other villages or to other masters their detainers being obligated, they shall be compelled to return to the abode of the desolated country districts. If their detainers should delay the execution of this regulation, they shall be liable to the fulfillment of the tax payment of such *homologi* and they shall restore to the masters whatever the masters prove that they have paid for such *homologi*.

4. Other flourishing villages shall be substituted in place of

* Protection, Pharr.

**which the coloni who are admittedly liable to taxation are known to provide, Pharr.

*** Pharr translates the Latin *functiones publicas et liturgos* as "compulsory public services and the payment of State slaves"

those *metrocomiae* which have either been made destitute or emptied of their resources by the lapse of time.

C.J.XI 48, 19
Date: 491-581

Emperor Anastasius Augustus.

Some *coloni* are *adscripticii* and their *peculia* belong to the owners, whereas others who served as *coloni* for 30 years shall remain free, together with their property; however, they shall be bound to cultivate the land and pay taxes. It shall be of benefit to both sides, the landowner and the *colonus*.

C.J.XI 48,22
Date: 531 A.D.
Justinian to Julian Praetorian Prefect

As we know, Our justice stipulates that no one's status may be decided upon in advance on the basis of a statement or a written confession alone: further corroboration is required. We deem therefore that the lease contract in itself or a statement in writing are by no means sufficient to impose the status of *adscripticius* on any one person and that such written statement needs to be supported by something else such as a written certificate on the enrollment in its tax lists or something like that as prescribed by law. If difficulties should arise, it is better to prove a person's status with the number of documents so that the condition of free men does not become worse solely on the basis of an admission of a written statement. If only a written certificate is submitted, supported by admission or testimony, and neither is done under duress (then what if a lease contract is shown or some other official document signed and deposited in the archives purposing that someone was *adscripticius* ?), then between those two documents on the liability, a written certificate and statement, and an admission, one should place trust with what has been written and deposited among the documents.

C.J.XI 48,23
Date: 531-535 A.D.
Justinian to Praetorian Prefect Johannes

As it is inhuman to separate *adscripticii* from the estate on which they have been from the beginning as its integral parts and acquire *coloni* from the estate of others, thereby inflicting enormous damage on landowners abandoned by them, We order that those under the title of *adscripticii* cannot gain their freedom again, no matter how many years have elapsed or whether they engaged in some other business over an extended period of time, just as *curiales* cannot be relieved of that status after the expiration of the certain period of time. They shall remain *adscripticii* and shall be tied to the land. And if someone should escape or it should be learned of his intent to leave the estate and—following the example of a fugitive slave—to hide for some time by fraudulent means, he shall nevertheless retain such status together with his offspring, even if they are born on a different estate; likewise, he shall be held liable for taxes and shall have no right to be exempted from any one of them. Just as Anastasius' law had decreed that persons who were retained by their condition of *coloni* for 30 years shall remain free but with no right to depart and move to another estate and request that the *colonus'* children, regardless of their sex, are also to be *coloni,* if their father was bound by this condition for 30 years, even though they themselves have not spent 30 years on the estate or in the village. We order that the *colonus'* children shall remain forever free as in the said law, but with no right to move elsewhere, abandoning the land on which they were born; they shall always remain bound to the estate which their parents agreed once to cultivate.

And the owners of the land on which such *coloni* happen to live themselves shall abstain from introducing a novelty or using violence. If such case should be proven or reported to the judge, the governor of the province in which this happened, shall examine it and shall redress the injustice if it has indeed taken place and shall see to it that the old custom of paying what is due is respected.

However, even in such cases the *coloni* shall not be permitted to leave the estate they live on. This shall apply equally to *coloni* and their children of any sex and any age; all those born on the estate shall remain on it in the same manner and under the same conditions under which their fathers remained on anothers' land.

Furthermore, no one shall be permitted to admit consciously and deliberately under his authority another person's *adscripticius* or *colonus.* If he should do so on trust and should discover subsequently, whether through admonition by landlord or by the owner of the *adscripticius* in person or through his *procurator* that he belongs to another, he shall return him together with his property and progeny. Should he fail to do that, he shall assume all tax liabilities, both for the land and for the cattle, for the whole period of time during which the fugitive *colonus* remained with him. Our very Eminent Prefecture and the governor of the province shall take care of that; they shall force them to return the fugitive *colonus* in keeping with old laws and shall have the latter punished.

SELECT BIBLIOGRAPHY

B. Adams, *Parmone und verwandte Text, Studien zum Dienstvertrag im Rechte der Papyri.* (Cologne 1964).

Akten VII Pap.Kongr. = *Akten des VII Papyrologischen Kongresses.* (Vienna 1955).

Atti XVII Pap.Congr. = *Atti del XVII congresso intern.di papirologia, I-III.* (Naples 1984).

T.D. Barnes, *The New Empire of Diocletian and Constantine.* Harvard, 1982.

H. Bolkstein, "De colonatu romano eiusque origine," Diss. Amsteloduni.1906.

H. Braunert, *Binnenwanderung* = *Binnenwanderung. Studien zur Sozialgeschichte in der Ptolemaeer - und Kaiserzeit.* (Bonn 1964).

N. Brockmeyer, Der Kolonat bei römischen Juristen der republikanischen und augusteischen Zeit, *Historia* 20:1971m732 ff.

J.M.Carié, Le colonat du Bas-Empire: un mythe historiographique, *Opus 1* (1982): 351 ff.

———— Un roman des origines: les généalogies du colonat du Bas-Empire, *Opus 2* (1983):205 ff.

A. Cerati, *Caractère annonaire et assiette de l'impôt foncier au Bas-Empire.* Bibliothèque d'histoire du droit et droit romain XX (Paris 1975)

Clausing, *Colonate* = R. Clausing, *The Roman Colonate, the theories of its origins.* (New York, 1925 [1965]).

P. Collinet, *La politique de Justinian à l'egard des colons.* Atti V. Congr. Intern. di studi bizantine. (Roma 1939), 600 ff.

A. Déléage, *La capitation du Bas-Empire.* (Maçon 1945).

E. Demougeot, A propos des lètes gaulois du IV siecle, Festschrift F. Altheim II, (1970) 101 ff.

———— *Modalités* d'établissement des fédérés de Gratien et de Théodose. Mélanges d'histoire ancienne offert à William Seston. (Paris 1974) 143 ff.

Eibach, *Kolonat* = D. Eibach, *Untersuchungen zum spätantiken Kolonat in der kaiserlichen Gesetzgebung, Cologne 1976.*

Finley, *Debt bondage* = M. Finley "Debt Bondage and the Problem of Slavery," *Revue hist. De droit français et etranger* 43 (1965):159 ff. = Economy and society in Ancient Greece, London 1980, 150 ff.

Fustel de Coulanges, *Colonat* = N.D. Fustel de Coulanges, *Le colonat romain, Recherches sur quelques problèmes d'histoire.* (Paris 1885).

L. Ganshof, "Le statut personnel du colon au Bas-Empire, observations en marge d' une théorie nouvelle," *Ant. Class.* 14 (1945):261 ff.

G. Garnsey, "Non slave Labour in the Roman World," *Proceedings Cambr. Philol. Soc.*, Suppl.6, (Cambridge, 1980): 47 ff.

J. Cascou, "Les grands domaines, la cité et l'état en Egypte byzantine," *Travaux et mémoires,* College de France, Centre de recherche d'histoire et civilisation de Byzance, 9, (1985); 1ff.

Gelzer, *Studien* = M. Gelzer, *Studien zur byzantinischen Verwaltung Ägyptens.* Leipziger hist. Abhandlungen, IIII, (Leipzig 1909).

Goffart, *Caput and Colonate* = W. Goffart, *Caput and Colonate, towards a History of Late Roman Taxation.* (Toronto 1974).

Hardy, *Larges estates* = E.R. Hardy, *The large Estates of Byzantine Egypt.* (New York 1931).

L. Harmand, *Libanius, Discours sur les patronage, texte traduit, annoté et commenté.* (Paris 1959).

W. Held, "Das Ende der progressiven Entwicklung des Kolonates am Ende des 2. und in der ersten Hälfte des 3. Jhds. im Römischen Imperium." *Klio* 52, (1970):239 ff.

K-P. Johne, J. Kuhn, V.Weber, *Die Kolonen in Italien und in den westlichen Provinzen des römischen Reiches.* (Berlin 1983).

A.H.M. Jones, "Census Records of the Later Roman Empire." *JRS* 43, (1953):228 ff.

―――― , *Colonate,* = "The Roman Colonate," *Past and Present* 13, (1957): 1ff.= P.A. Brunt, *The Roman Economy.* (1974), ch.XV,293 ff.

―――― , "Capitatio and Iugatio," *JRS* 47, (1957): 88 ff.

―――― , *Idem,* LRE = *The Later Roman Empire.* I-II, (London 1973).

A.Ch. Johnson, *Roman Egypt to the Reign of Diocletian,* in Tenney Frank ESAR II (*An Economic Survey of Ancient Rome*) 1936.

Kaser, *Privatrecht* = M.Kaser, *Das römische Privatrecht, Erster Abscnitt: Das Altrömische, das vorklassische und klassische Recht.* (Münich 1971) *zweite, neubearbeitet Auflage; II. Zweite Abschnitt: die nachklassischen Entwicklungen, zweite neubearbeitete Auflage* (Münich 1975).

J.G. Keenan, "On Law and Society in Late Roman Egypt," *ZPE* 17/3, (1975): 237 ff.

D. Kehoe, "Risk and Investment on the Estates of Pliny," *Chiron* 18, (1988): 26ff.

J. Kolendo, *Le colonat en Afrique sous le Haut-Empire.* Centre de recherches d'histoire ancienne 17, Annales litteraires de l'Université de Besançon, 1977.

A.V. Koptev, "Svoboda" I "repostvo" kolonov v pozdnei Rimskoi imperii ("The Freedom and Slavery of the *coloni in the Later*

Roman Empire"), *VDI* (1990/2): 24 ff.

W. Kunkel, *Auctoratur,* Symbolae Taubenschlag dedicatae III, 207 ff.= Eos 47,1957.

E. Léotard, Essai sur la condition des barbares établis dans l'Empire romain (thèse), *1873.*

N. Lewis. *The Romanity of Roman Egypt,* Atti XVII Pap. Congr. 1984,III 1077 ff.

A. Marcone, *De colonato tardoantico nella storiografia moderna, da Fustel de Coulanges ai nostri giorni,* (Bibliotheca di Athenaeum 7, 1988).

M. Mirkovič, *Flucht der Bauern, Fiskal-und Privatschulden,* Studien zur Geschichte der römischen Spätantike, Festgabe für Professor Johannes Straub, (Bonn 1989), 147 ff.

————, Ὑπήκοοι und σύμμαχοι, *Ansiedlung und Rekrutierung von Barbaren bis zum Jahr 382,* Klassische Altertum, Spätantike und frühes Christentum, Adolf Lippold sum 65.Geburgtstag gewidmet, (Würzburg 1993),425 ff.

Mitteis, *Grundzüge,* = L. Mitteis, *Grundzüge und Chrestomatie der Papyruskunde,* II, *erste Hälfte"* Grumdzüge. zweite Hälfte, Chrestomatie. (Berlin 1912).

Reichsrecht = L.Mitteis, Reichsrecht und Voksrecht in den östlichen Provinzen des römischen Kaiserreiches. (Leipzig 1891).

R. MacMullen, "Social Mobility and the Theodosian Code," *JRS* 54, (1964): 49 ff.

Th. Mommsen, "Bürgerlicher und peregrinischer," *Freicheitschutz irn römischen Staat, Juristische Abhandlungen, Festgabe für Georg Beseler zum 6. Januar,* Berlin (1885), 258 ff . Ges.Schr. III,P.L ff.

O. Montevecchi, *11 contrati di lavoro e di servizio nell' Egitto greco-romano,* Milano 1950.

P.W. de Neeve, *Colonus. Private Farm tenancy in Roman Italy during the Republic and the Early Principate,* Amsterdam 1982.

D. Nörr, "Zur sozialen und rechtlichen Bewertung der freien Arbeit in Rom," *ZSS* 82 (1965): 86 ff.

Palasse, *Orient et Occident* = M. Palasse, *Orient et Occident à propos du colonat romain au Bas-Empire,*1950.

C. Pharr, *The Theodosian Code and Novels and the girmondian Constitutiones, a translation with commentary, glossary and bibliography,* New York, 1952.

Preisigke, Wörterbuch =   F. Preisigke, *Wörterbuch der griechischen Papyruskunden mit Einfluss der griecheschen Inschriften, Aufschriften, Ostraka, Mumienschilden usw. aus Egypten,* I-II, Berlin,1927; III. *Besondere Wörterliste,* bearb. von E.Kiessling, Berlin,

1931.

   Proceed. XVI Pap.Kongr. =   *Proceedings of the XVII Inter.*
Congress of Papyrology, Chicago, 1981.

   P. Rosafio, *Inquilinus,* opus 3,(1984),121 ff.

   Rostowzew, Kolonat   =   M. Rostowzew,   *Studien zur*
Geschichte der römischen Kolonatus, Archiv für Papyrusforschung.
Beiheft 1, Leipzig und Berlin, 1910.

   Saumagne, *Origo* =   Ch. Saumagne, "Du rôle de l'origo' et du
'census' dans la formation du colonat romain," *Byzantion* 12 (1937):
487 ff.

   F.C. Savigny, *Über dem römischen Kolonat.* Vermischte
schriften II, (Berlin 1850) 1 ff.

   Seeck, *Untergang* = O. Seeck, *Geschichte des Untergangs der*
antiken Welt I-V, (Berlin 1901-1913).

   Segrè, *Colonate* = A. Segrè, "The Byzantine Colonate," *Trad-*
itio 5, (1947): 103 ff.

   B. Sirks, "Reconsidering the Roman Colonate," *ZSS* RA 110,
(1993): 330 ff.

   Stein, *Bas-Empire* = E. Stein, *Histoire du Bas-Empire.* (Amsterdam 1968).

   R.Taubenschlag, *The Law of Greco-Roman Egypt in the Light of*
the Papyri, 332 BC - 640 AD. (Warszawa.1955).

   D.Thomas, "A Petition to the Prefect of Egypt and related
Imperial Edicts." *JEA* 61, (1975): 201 ff.

   J. Triantaphyllopoulos,   (P.Oxy.2479) *REG* 80, (1967):353ff.

   Wessely, *Stud.pal.* = C. Wessely, Studien zur Palaeography und
Papyruskunde I. (1903).

   Wilcken, *Grundzüge* = U.Wilcken, *Grundzüge; und Chresto-*
matie der Papyruskunde I, ersher Hälfte: zweite Hälfte: Chrestomatie.
(Berlin 1912).

   S. Zulueta, *De patrociniis vicorum,* in Vinogradoff, Oxford
Studies in Social and Legal History, I,2, (1909).

INDEX

Index (Greek)

www.ingramcontent.com/pod-product-compliance
Lightning Source LLC
Chambersburg PA
CBHW080928100426
42812CB00007B/2401